Advent and Christmas in a Catholic Home

By Helen McLaughlin

First edited by
Christopher & Katherine Zehnder
1994 – St. Raphael Press

Artwork by Katherine Zehnder

Updated and revised 2019 by Clotilde Zehnder

Copyright © 2019 by Savage Mountain Press

ISBN 978-1-7342519-0-6

Table of Contents

Editor's introduction.. i
The Season of Grace and Joy.. 1
Advent Wreath 5
The Empty Manger 9
Advent Prayers.. 9
Advent Hymns 11
The Jesse Tree 16
St. Nicholas Day 18
The Christ Candle 22
Mary's Candle.. 22
Our Lady of Guadalupe... 24
St. Lucy 28
Advent Ember Days... 29
Christmas Manger 32
The Advent House 32
Tree Decorations 35
Christmas Cooking 35
Christmas 43
Blessing of The Tree 49
Morning Prayers during The Christmas Season........................ 51
Evening Prayers during the Christmas Season 53
Caroling... 56
St. Stephen, December 26 62
St. John, Apostle and Evangelist, December 27....................... 63
Holy Innocents, December 28 64
Feast of the Holy Family, December 30 67
Solemnity of Mary, Mother of God... 69
Epiphany 72
Epiphany Evening Prayers... 76
Feasts of The Epiphany Season 82
St. Brigid.. 83
Feast of The Presentation 84
Resources 87
Book List 89
Index of Recipes (alphabetical) 91
Index of Recipes (by feast) 92
Index of Songs (alphabetical) 94
Index of Songs (by feast) 95

"Behold the handmaid of the Lord;
be it done to me according to thy word."

—— Lk. 1:38

Editor's introduction

Advent and Christmas in a Catholic Home is a compilation of two small books written by Helen McLoughlin in the 1950's: *Family Advent Customs* and *Christmas to Candlemas in a Catholic Home* (both originally published by The Liturgical Press, St. John's Abbey, Collegeville, MN). I had seen *Family Advent Customs* in my father's hands during my childhood and fortunately came across it years later in his library. It seemed to me a treasure, sent to aid me in enriching my own young children's spiritual lives. We knew other parents were also looking for such help, and so we decided to share Mrs. McLoughlin's wisdom and experience with them.

Mrs. McLoughlin's children attended Catholic schools at a time when Catholic education was strong and true to her mission; yet, even then Mrs. McLoughlin did not assume this to be enough or presume her parental task complete. The McLoughlins' home life was rich in prayer and ceremony, celebrating with the Church her liturgical seasons and feasts. How much more should we strive in a time of cultural and moral chaos and attack on the Church and family to create such a spiritual environment in our homes and communities. No amount of doctrinal instruction will make the faith seem as true and alive as will a beautiful liturgy, a solemn ceremony, a mother's care in preparing special feast day meals, or night prayers in candlelight followed by a goodnight hymn and a father's blessing. It is daily events such as these that our children will most remember as adults and that will form and reinforce their Catholic culture.

For we learn best those lessons that are grasped with the senses as well as our intellect. Pope Pius XI wrote: "…people are instructed in the truths of faith and brought to appreciate the inner joys of religion far more effectively by the annual celebration of our sacred mysteries than by any official pronouncement of the teaching Church. Such pronouncements usually reach only a few and the more learned among the faithful; feasts reach them all. The Church's teaching affects the mind primarily; her feasts affect both mind and heart and have a salutary effect upon man's whole nature." Thus the Church in her Founder's wisdom has taught us through Easter candlelight in a dark church, an empty tabernacle on Good Friday, a bishop's "slap" on a confirmandee's cheek, as well as through the simple creations of incense, water, bells, candles, food and music. This learning seems especially suited to young children with their keen desire to touch, hear, and see the opening world about them. It is best then to feed their sensitive souls with all that is good and beautiful in the natural world that they may thereby come to love Goodness and Beauty Himself.

This book will hopefully aid parents in the great responsibility Our Lord has given them to provide a fertile and nourishing soil wherein the seed of faith can sprout and mature into a tree that will yield an abundance of good fruit.

Note: The mass Mrs. McLaughlin attended was that of the Traditional Latin Rite, now called the Extraordinary Form of the Roman Rite. The feasts mentioned in her book (except for Our Lady of Guadalupe, a new feast) were celebrated according to the calendar of that rite. Since then, many feast days have been moved or removed and some liturgical customs - such as ember days - dropped. For those who attend a parish where the Extraordinary Form of the Mass is celebrated and use its liturgical calendar, this should present no difficulties; those who attend the Ordinary Form will have to make adjustments according to the common liturgical calendar.

The original copies of Mrs. McLaughlin's books contained many charming photographs of her family exemplifying their practice of these Advent and Christmas customs. These photos were unfortunately not reproducible, but we hope you will get a good sense of her spirit without them. We give special thanks to William McLoughlin for his kind cooperation in helping us to make his late wife's books again available to Catholic families.

The Season of Grace and Joy

Christmas is a liturgical season of great joy. It lasts forty days, from December 25 to February 2, during which the birth of Jesus Christ our Savior is celebrated as one continuous festival. The finale comes with His presentation in the temple. A season most dear to Christian hearts, Christmas is as distinct in the liturgy as Advent, Lent, Easter, or Pentecost. Four weeks of Advent are scarcely enough to "prepare the way of the Lord" for His coming to us as King. However, if we have used that season as a preparation, we are ready now to receive the Redeemer who will deliver us from sin in answer to our requests. Christ's coming must be not a lovely idyll or a pastoral scene, but a reality accomplished in our lives and our children's. Forty days of rejoicing are not too long a celebration for so great an event.

The early Church selected December 25, the date of the winter solstice when God the Creator gives the sun an increase of natural light in northern hemispheres, as the day on which to celebrate the birth of the Sun of Justice, Light of the world. Radiating from the Divine Child are a galaxy of wonderful saints whose lives afford a continuing interest in celebrating the feast of His birth.

Micheas, who lived in the days of Isaias, prophesied the birthplace of the Messiah: "Thou, Bethlehem, art a little one among the thousands in Judah; out of thee shall He come forth unto me that is to be the Ruler of Israel; and His going forth is from the beginning, from the days of eternity." The name Bethlehem signifies House of Bread. To it at Christmas comes the Savior, who is the Bread of Life. By our participation in this mystery the divine transformation takes place whereby He "reshapes the body of our lowliness after the body of His splendor."

Our forbearers gave the name Christmas to the feast of our Lord's birth because they kept the "Christ Mass" as the heart of their celebrations. Following closely the liturgy of the Church, they centered their customs and wrote their hymns and carols on her practices of the season, adoration, love, joy, and gratitude. Those practices also increased their admiration for His Virgin Mother Mary, who gave Almighty God His human form. He had created heaven and earth by His Word, but His becoming Man depended on a creature's FIAT, *Be it done unto me according to Thy Word.* Mary consented. Our forebearers honored her in their great masterpieces because she is God's Mother. For the same reason the world in our day honors her as Queen of Heaven.

It is to Our Lady that Christian families must look for help to reestablish Christmas as a season of festivities marking Christ's birth. Either we live the liturgical year with its varying seasons of joy and sorrow, work and rest, or we follow the pattern of the world. Nor is it an easy task to break with the world and the powerful influence of advertising. Their season of Christmas begins around Thanksgiving Day when stores display wares for holiday gift-giving. It lasts until December 24.

Families, who would not dream of eating their Thanksgiving turkey a week in advance or of having their 4th of July picnic in June, give no thought to the fact that, when they awake on December 25, there is not a shred of Christmas left. Every present has been opened. Every carol has been sung. The tree has dried out. Christmas is apt to be a dull day given to over-eating. There was no fast in Advent, so it follows that there can be no feast.

It is difficult to keep one's home dark in Advent penance; to keep a tree fresh outside the door; to refrain from singing carols until Christmas eve. Our children see their friends' trees shimmering with ornaments a week before Christmas. Their houses are bedecked with lights. Television and radio blare carols. Not only is it difficult to keep from celebrating beforehand, it is even more difficult to begin forty days of the Christmas season when all around people are concluding their festivities. How then do families return to the spirit of the Church and begin the season of joy and grace on Christmas eve?

The simplest way is by keeping Advent. Advent is the beginning of the new liturgical year. It is a season of spiritual reparation, marked by eager longing for the coming of the Savior through grace at Christmas, and for His second and final coming. It is also an ideal time to establish in our homes liturgical customs which will restore our children to Christ.

In our family we use these age-old Advent practices to help our children live closer to Christ and His Church during the pre-Christmas season. Time-tested and proven, the customs teach the doctrines of redemption and develop a generosity with God and a coordination of the family's spiritual efforts as effectively now as they did for our forebears. Their strong and living faith will be the heritage of our children if family religious practices, centered in the Liturgy, "The Normal School of Sanctity for the Laity," are established in our homes.

Secularism has invaded our households. The Bishops of the United States have warned us that "The Christian must make his home holy – the Christian must realize the Christian ideal." Father Edgar Schmiedler, O.S.B., in his three excellent pamphlets, *Your Home A Church in Miniature*, says of family customs and blessings: "They are a relatively simple, but highly important, means of union between altar and home. They are a media for channeling from one great spiritual reservoir, given into the Church's keeping by Christ, the living and transforming waters of grace from the Savior's fountain."

Children love to anticipate. When there are empty mangers to fill with straws of small sacrifices, when the Mary-Candle is a daily reminder on the dinner table, when Advent hymns are sung in the candlelight of a graceful Advent wreath, children are not anxious to celebrate Christmas before time. That would offend their sense of honor. Older children who make Nativity sets, cut Old Testament symbols to decorate a Jesse tree, or prepare costumes for a Christmas play will find Advent all too short a time to prepare for the coming of Christ the King.

Children, who love the beauty and simplicity of family religious practices, make the traditions easy to establish. As a rule it is best to begin with one or two customs and others in years to come. It is also highly desirable that families develop their own special customs, at least by adapting traditional ones to their personal circumstances. Once established, customs recall to older members of the family long-forgotten practices of their own childhood. These have a special appeal because they belonged to our forefathers and link us to the wealth of national customs now fallen into disuse.

Celebrating Christmas in its season can be accomplished more easily when several families try it together. Frequently there are families who, if only for sentimental reasons, would like to keep the joy and surprise of Christmas for the eve. Christians of the Eastern rite wait until their particular feast of Christmas comes in January. We should likewise begin ours on its proper day. We also need time for our festivities. As difficult as it may be, we should decline invitations to celebrate Christmas at the various parties sprinkled throughout the Advent season. The Church gives us a period of forty days for rejoicing. Instead, invite friends and family to your own joyous celebration of Christ's birth during the many days following December 25th, when for others it is otherwise a disappointing and barren time.

Archbishop Richard J. Cushing of Boston, in urging Christian parents to establish family practices said, "This is what the Church expects of you in Advent. She invites you to look through the eyes of faith, upon the world, upon the invisible growth of a land of inexhaustible riches, wherein the Sower of Life unites humanity to divinity. If during Advent we open our souls fully, the Heavens will rain the Just One."

St. Pius X, whose burning desire was to restore all things to Christ, might well become the patron of parents who wish to restore their children to Christ through these practices. Our Blessed Lady and St. Joseph too will send inspiration from the Holy Spirit, for theirs was a home where feast day cooking, family customs, family prayers and singing abounded, according to prescribed Jewish law. It is to them we must look for help in order to train our children "to live temporarily, justly, reverently, in this world, awaiting the Advent of the glory of the great God."

We await a Savior,
The Lord Jesus Christ,
Who will reshape the body
  of our lowliness
After the shape of the body
  of His splendour.
Temperately, justly, reverently,
Let us live
  in this world,
Awaiting the blessed hope
And advent of the glory
  of the great God.
— Responsory in Advent

Advent Wreath

Most popular of the Advent customs handed down to us is the Advent wreath, made of evergreens, bound to a circle of wire. German in origin – it was taken, so we are told, from the pagan fire wheel – the wreath represents the cycle of thousands of years from Adam to Christ during which the world awaited the coming of a Redeemer. It also represents the cycle of years since then that we have been awaiting His second and final coming in glory. It bears four candles, equally spaced, three purple ones to be lighted on the "penitential" Sundays, and a pink one for *Gaudete*, the joyful Sunday in Advent. Candles may be placed inside or outside the wreath.

Any kind of Christmas wreath such as those hung in windows may be used. It may be set on a kitchen or dining room table, on an end table in the living room, or in a child's bedroom. However, it is most appealing when suspended by four purple ribbons from a light fixture in the ceiling.

When our children were small we bought a large, permanently preserved pine wreath and used it year after year. Now that they are going to school they help make a new one each Advent. Inexpensive and easy to assemble is the wreath we make from a bunch or two of laurel leaves bound to a circle of wire from coat hangers. The evergreens are secured by fine wire to the circle. Candles and ribbons are added as the wreath is put together. Laurel is practical because it does not shed when suspended over the dining room table. Moreover, laurel is a symbol of victory, and thus reminds us that Christ's coming means victory over sin and death.

Loveliest of wreaths and fragrant, too, is one of fresh princess pine. When we use that type, we hang it in the living room and add a single silver star to it each evening in Advent when the candles are lighted for prayers.

The home ceremony for use of the Advent wreath is simple. It consists of the Collect for the Sundays of the season. On the first Sunday of Advent, the family gathers for the blessing of the wreath by the father, who begins:

Father: Our help is in the Name of the Lord.
All answer: Who made heaven and earth.
Father: Let us pray. O God, by whose Word all things are sanctified, pour forth Thy blessing upon this wreath, and grant that we who use it may prepare our hearts for the coming of Christ and may receive from Thee abundant graces. Through Christ our Lord,
All: Amen.

The father sprinkles the wreath with holy water. Then the youngest child lights the first candle, and the prayer for the first week is said.

Father: Let us pray. Sir up Thy might, we beg Thee, O Lord, and come, so that we may escape through Thy protection and be saved by Thy help from the dangers that threaten us because of our sins. Who livest and reignest for ever and ever,
All: Amen.

During the first week one candle is left burning during the evening meal, at prayers, or at bedtime.

Two candles are lighted on the second Sunday and allowed to burn as before. The prayer for the week is:

Father: Let us pray. O Lord, stir up our hearts that we may prepare for Thy only begotten Son, that through His coming we may be made worthy to serve Thee with pure souls. Through the same Christ our Lord,
All: Amen.

Three candles are lighted on the third Sunday and during that week. The prayer is:

Father: Let us pray. We humbly beg Thee, O Lord, to listen to our prayers; and by the grace of Thy coming bring light into our darkened minds. Who livest and reignest for ever and ever,
All: Amen.

All four candles are lighted on the fourth Sunday and allowed to burn as before. The prayer said the fourth week is:

Father: Let us pray. Stir up Thy might, we pray Thee, O Lord, and come; rescue us through Thy great strength so that salvation, which has been hindered by our sins, may be hastened by the grace of Thy gentle mercy. Who livest and reignest for ever and ever.
All: Amen.

Plum Pudding

On the first Sunday of Advent we bring to the dinner table the "Stir-up" or traditional English plum pudding for family and guests to stir. They make a wish as they stir and then pray the Collect from the Mass of the day:

> "Stir up Thy might, we beg Thee, O Lord, and come so that we may escape through Thy protection and be saved by Thy help from the dangers that threaten us because of our sins. Who livest and reignest for over and ever."

Afterwards the pudding is steamed and put away until the feast of Christmas when it returns in a blaze of brandy to the dinner table. Actually the pudding is prepared on the Saturday before "Stir-up" Sunday. Filled with the good things of the world, the pudding is supposed to represent Christ who will bring with Him on His birthday all the good things of heaven. Children love to work on the pudding, and the busy mother finds extra hands a great help in dicing, grating and juicing the fruits.

We use a recipe from *Jubilee*, November 1953. The ingredients make five pounds of pudding. Adolph Paganuzzi, chef of a well-known Greenwich Village, New York, pastry shop, reduced his famous recipe to family proportions for *Jubilee*. With his kind permission we give it here:

½ lb. beef suet, chopped
¼ lb. all-purpose flour, sifted
¼ lb. bread crumbs
¾ lb. brown sugar
2 tsp. ground cinnamon
1 tsp. ground allspice
1 tsp. ground ginger
¼ lbs. raisins – any kind
¼ lb. diced candied citron
¼ lb. diced candied orange peels
¼ lb. diced candied lemon peels
3 eggs, beaten
2 lemons – grated rind and their juice
2 oranges – grated rind and their juice
½ pt. sherry or port wine

In a bowl mix and work together all the ingredients one at a time, in the order in which they are listed above. When they are well combined, pour the mixture into a well-greased can (or other utensil), cover, and seal tight. Steam in large, covered kettle, roaster or similar utensil and let simmer for at least five hours. When done, the pudding can be stored away until Christmas. It may be kept a year and will improve with age. It may be served with any sauce desired, such as fruit, rum, brandy, raisin, vanilla or any other kind. Liquid sauces are better than semi-liquid.

Rum Sauce

1 pint sherry wine
½ lb. brown sugar
2 bay leaves
1 small stick cinnamon
Rind of ½ orange
½ pt. rum

Place all the ingredients in a glass jar and let stand together for a few days. Bring to a boil, strain and serve over the pudding.

The Empty Manger

On the first Sunday of Advent each child in our family receives an empty manger. A sugar box covered with bright paper will do as well. At bedtime the children draw straws for each kind deed performed in honor of Baby Jesus as His birthday surprise. The straws are placed in the child's manger or box daily. It is amazing how much love a child can put into Advent when he is preparing for His Redeemer's coming in grace.

On Christmas each child finds an Infant in his manger, placed on a small table or on a chair beside his bed. Usually it is a tiny doll, beautifully dressed; but one of our children receives a Hummel Infant year after year. This custom, which in no way interferes with the larger manger in the living room, fills the child with longing in Advent, and gives him an image of his Redeemer as his first happy glance mornings and his last impression at night during the entire Christmas season.

Advent Prayers

In order to correspond more closely to the mind of Holy Mother Church during this important season, our night prayers consist of the Mass Collect for the day, a psalm or reading from the Advent prophets, and an Advent hymn. Children particularly love psalms, once they have learned that they are the prayers our Lord Himself said when He was a boy on earth. One of the children's favorites is:

> O shepherd of Israel, hearken,
>   O guide of the flock of Joseph!
> Rouse your power,
>   and come to save us.
>   O Lord of hosts, restore us,
>   if your face shine upon us,
>   then we shall be safe.
> O Lord of hosts, how long will you burn with anger
>   while your people pray?
> You have fed them with the bread of tears
>   and given them tears to drink in ample measure.
> You have left us to be fought over by our neighbors,

>   and our enemies mock us.
>   O Lord of hosts, restore us.
>   if your face shine upon us,
>   then we shall be safe.

Another prayer children enjoy is a prophecy from Isaias. It refers to Christ as the Root of Jesse, the thirsty plant, in whose honor we use evergreens during Advent and Christmas. It also gives the genealogy of the Savior:

>   A Root shall come forth from the stock of Jesse
>   And a Flower shall rise out of his root!
>   And the spirit of the Lord shall rest upon Him —
>   the spirit of wisdom and of understanding,
>   the spirit of counsel and of fortitude,
>   the spirit of knowledge and of godliness.
>   The people that walked in darkness
>   shall see a great light,
>   For a Child is born to us
>   and a Son is given to us.
>   To Him all power shall be given.
>   His Name shall be: Wonderful One,
>   Strong God, Eternal One, Prince of Peace.
>   He shall sit on the throne of David,
>   And He will found a new Covenant
>   which will last for ever and ever.

Isaias also gives us two Advent prayers which are appropriate before grace at meals for this season. Mornings and at noon we use the versicle of Lauds "which is as it were spur making us conscious of the particular mystery of the season." Before grace the mother prays:

The voice of one crying in the wilderness: Prepare the way of the Lord.
All answer: Make straight His paths.

This is also the particular prayer we use in preparing each child for our Lord's coming in First Holy Communion. It is therefore especially dear to the family.

At the evening meal we use the Vespers versicle which is "a sedative, soothing our hearts in spiritual repose." Before grace the father says:

Drop down dew, ye heavens above, and let the clouds rain the Just One. *All answer:* Let the earth be opened and bud forth a Savior.

Here again the versicle is familiar because we sing the words in Latin during evening prayers.

Advent Hymns

Mother Church has wisely provided her children with Advent hymns. Favorites are the deeply moving *Rorate Coeli*, translated "Bedew us, heaven, from above," and "O Come, O Come Emmanuel." Our children sing these hymns at school. We have a little pump organ at home which they play. Frequently an inquiry will bring to light one covered with dust in a church basement or in the attic of a farm house. Nothing stimulates family hymn singing so much as an organ. It is a happy adjunct to the home that is a "church in miniature."

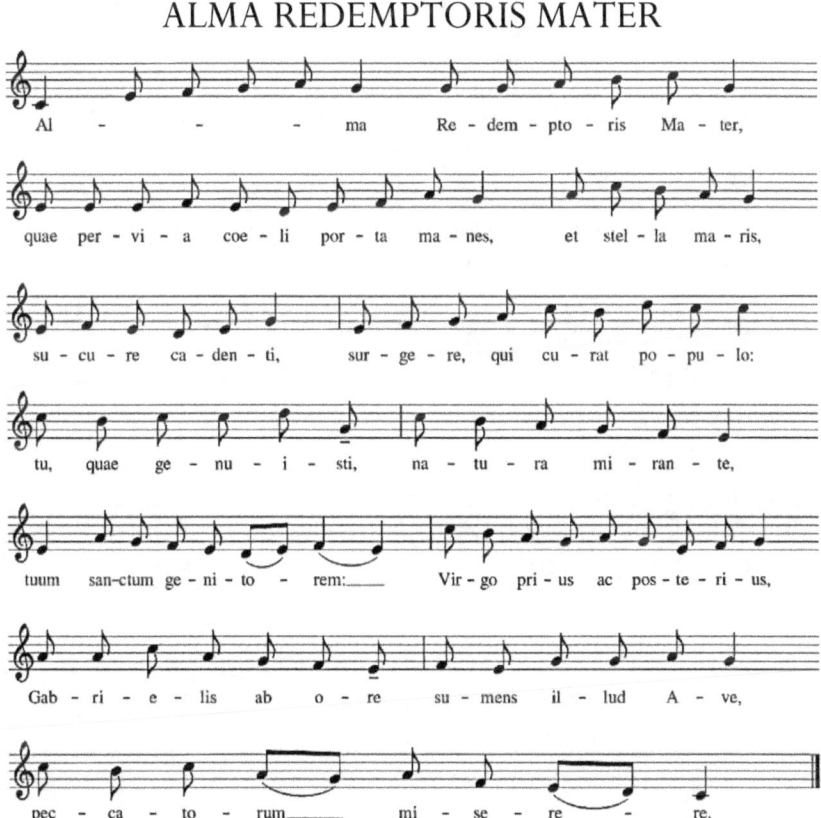

ALMA REDEMPTORIS MATER

O COME, O COME EMMANUEL

RORATE CAELI

GABRIEL'S MESSAGE

SAVIOR OF THE NATIONS COME

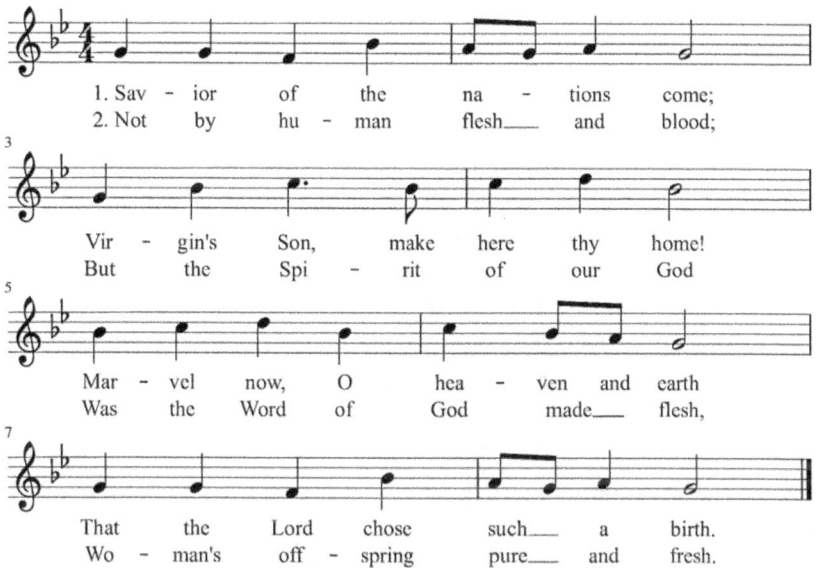

1. Sav-ior of the nations come;
   Virgin's Son, make here thy home!
   Marvel now, O heaven and earth
   That the Lord chose such a birth.

2. Not by human flesh and blood;
   But the Spirit of our God
   Was the Word of God made flesh,
   Woman's offspring pure and fresh.

3. Wondrous birth! O wondrous Child
   Of the Virgin undefiled!
   Though by all the world disowned,
   Still to be in heaven enthroned.

4. From the Father forth He came
   And returneth to the same,
   Captive leading death and hell –
   High the song of triumph swell!

5. Thou, the Father's only Son,
   Hast o'er sin the victory won.
   Boundless shall Thy kingdom be;
   When shall we its glories see?

6. Brightly doth Thy manger shine,
   Glorious is its light divine.
   Let not sin o'ercloud this light;
   Ever be our faith thus bright.

7. Praise to God the Father sing,
   Praise to God the Son, our King,
   Praise to God the Spirit be
   Ever and eternally.

The Jesse Tree

We first heard about the Jesse Tree in *Worship* magazine. It is an Advent custom which is especially good for younger children who learn and easily grasp stories through pictures. The Jesse Tree tells of the ancestry of Jesus through symbols and relates the scriptural story of our redemption - the purpose of Christ's coming - from Creation to the Birth of the Promised Messiah. A Jesse Tree can be cut from any large sheet of paper or cardboard to resemble a tree, making sure it is large enough to accommodate all the symbols. A Jesse Tree can also be made by using a small potted leafless tree or branch. At the base or trunk of our Jesse Tree we write these verses from Isaias: "There shall come forth a shoot from the stump of Jesse, and a branch shall grow out of his roots. And the Spirit of the Lord shall rest upon him, the spirit of wisdom and understanding, the spirit of counsel and might, the spirit of knowledge and the fear of the Lord." The tree represents the Root of Jesse and is decorated with homemade symbols depicting the ancestors of Jesus or Old Testament events leading to Him.

After the symbol is explained to the children and the related scriptural passages read (older children, more familiar with the Bible, may be able to find the corresponding stories themselves), the children draw or make from clay or "dough" the symbol to be hung for the clay. Materials found around the house -such as toothpicks, felt, foil, buttons – as well as old calendars and magazines can be used. For Adam and Eve we use a rosy apple with two bites taken from it; for Abraham and Isaac, a ram; for Solomon, a temple; for Moses, two tablets of the Law; for David, a star; for Isaias, a hand with a burning coal. These were drawn by an artist friend and cut by the children from bright paper. Freehand, we cut a pitcher from silver paper to symbolize Rebecca, using a milk jug from Williamsburg as a model. We also cut shells for John the Baptist and sheaves of wheat for Ruth. The children helped their father make a ladder and attach to its rungs tiny angels to symbolize Jacob. We placed a crown bearing twelve stars for our Lady at the top of the tree and above the crown a rose for Our Savior who budded from the Root of Jesse. To these we added beautiful hand-carved wooden "O" antiphons and symbols of our Savior made by the Benedictine nuns at Regina Laudis, Bethlehem, Connecticut. These same symbols can also be made as Christmas tree decorations.

Here are a few suggestions for your Jesse Tree:

Creation: any symbol from the six days, such as the sun, moon, stars, plants, birds, fish, mammals, Adam and Eve. If more symbols are needed in order to complete the number of days in Advent this is the best area to add them. There is an interesting further symbolism of the sun and moon: the sun representing Christ who gives light to the world; and the moon, representing Our Lady who reflects the light of Christ

The Fall: an apple, apple tree
Noah: an ark, rainbow
Abraham: staff and sandals, tent
Isaac: bundle of sticks, knife, lamb
Rebecca: silver pitcher, well
Jacob: ladder
Joseph: coat of many colors
Moses: burning bush, tablets of 10 commandments
Samuel: scrolls
Jesse: flowering rod
Ruth: sheaves of wheat
David: harp, slingshot, Star of David
Solomon: throne, sword, scales of Justice, temple of Jerusalem
Isaiah: pincers and red coal
Anne and Joachim: golden gates of Jerusalem, basket of doves
Zachary and Elizabeth: thurible, slateboard
John the Baptist: long slender staff tipped with a cross, platter and sword, the River Jordon, shell
Joseph: carpenter's tools
Mary: lily, crown with twelve stars
The Nativity: donkey, star, angel
Christ: Chi-Rho, rose

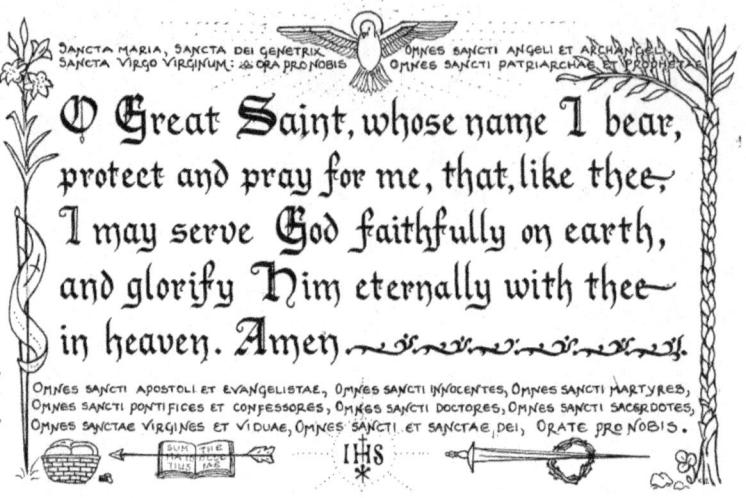

St. Nicholas Day

V: *The Lord led the just man in right paths*
R: *And showed him the kingdom of God,*
Ant: *The Lord loved him and adorned him;*
He clothed him with splendid apparel,
and crowned him at the gates of paradise
- from Vespers of St, Nicholas

St. Nicholas' feast day, December 6, is one of the highlights of the Advent season. It is on this eve that our children hang their stockings. From babyhood they learn to love the kind bishop with his miter, staff, and bag of gifts, whose name has become parodied as "Santa Claus" and whose memory is tarnished by commercialism, In addition to the toys received on this feast, the Christ Child and His angels bring other gifts on Christmas Eve. It is also a custom for children to put out their shoes on the eve of St. Nicholas so that the saint can fill them with treats. Many families like to leave refreshments for the saint and his helpers: a glass of milk or a cold beer for the bishop, a cookie for his helper Peterbaas, and a carrot for the donkey.

Placing less exclusive emphasis on December 25 as the day of presents and also curtailing its gifts somewhat makes it easier to place more emphasis on the religious aspects of that great holy day. Do other children think ours are strange? Not at all. If anything, they are a bit envious of children who receive Yule gifts so early and who enjoy such a happy feast as our traditional St.

Nicholas Day party. Having an early gift day also makes it possible for the children to give some of these gifts as Christmas presents to other less fortunate children.

Treats of the St. Nicholas party are the exchange of gifts, genuine Dutch cookies and Bishopwyn (bishop's wine). For the children the wine is grape juice. But the grown-ups who face the high December winds along the Hudson River to pick up their children at our house always welcome the mulled Bishopwyn. Its recipe is from our favorite cookbook, *Cooking for Christ* by Florence Berger.

Bishopwyn

1 bottle of Claret
6 cloves
4" stick cinnamon

Break cinnamon into small pieces. Simmer wine and spices for about five minutes. Strain wine, serve hot.

This next recipe is the traditional rolled cookies made in Holland for St. Nicholas Day. Cookies can be cut in the shape of a bishop's miter, a bishop or a donkey (St. Nicholas's beast of burden when he delivers gifts) or in the shape of the traditional Christmas stocking. One could also use gingerbread boy or girl cookie cutters in honor of the patron saint of children.

❖❖❖

Speculaas Cookies

1 cup butter
2 cups brown dark brown sugar
2 eggs
Zest of 1 lemon
2 tsp. cinnamon
1 tsp. ground nutmeg

½ tsp. ground cloves
1/8 tsp. ground ginger
1/8 tsp. salt
4 cups flour
1 tsp. baking powder

Icing (optional)

Cream the butter and sugar. Add eggs one at a time and blend thoroughly after each addition. Add lemon zest. Combine dry ingredients and gradually combine with butter mixture. Form dough into a disc, wrap in wax paper or plastic wrap and chill several hours or overnight. Bring back to room temperature and roll out dough on floured surface to 1/8 inch. Cut out with cookie cutters. Bake on lightly greased baking sheets for 10 to 12 minutes at 350°. Optional: paint cookies with colored icing when cooled.

❖❖❖

According to legend, St. Nicholas threw a bag or purse of coins three times into the window of a poor man to provide dowries for each of his three daughters. These cookies remind us of St. Nicholas's love for the poor.

St. Nicholas' Purse Cookies

½ (one stick) butter, softened
¼ cup packed brown sugar
¼ cup granulated sugar
1 egg
1 teaspoon vanilla extract
1 ½ cups all-purpose flour
¼ cup cornstarch
½ teaspoon baking soda
¼ teaspoon salt
24 pieces of chocolate candy (such as Hershey's Kisses) or other candy about the same size that can be baked.

Preheat oven to 350. In a large bowl, cream together butter and sugars. Add the egg and beat until fluffy. Stir in vanilla. Combine the flour, cornstarch, baking soda, and salt. Stir into the butter mixture. Beat until it forms a ball. Divide the dough into 24 pieces. Roll each piece into a ball. Press a candy into the center of each ball and mold the dough up around the candy to form a "bag." If it looks like your bag may burst, add more dough (making fewer bags). Place bags on ungreased cookie sheet and bake for 10 minutes or until lightly browned. Let the bags cool slightly on the cookie sheet before moving them to a rack to cool completely. Cookies can be dusted in powdered sugar. They also can be decorated with icing to mimic the look of a cinched bag.

These cookies can also be made more quickly with puff pastry. Roll out thawed pastry and cut in 2" – 3" circles. Place the candy in the center of each and fold the pastry up to form a bag. Bake according to the directions for puff pastry.

❖❖❖

During the party we light the Advent wreath candles, and the children sing Advent hymns. All classes at Corpus Christi School have wreaths, but many of the children do not have them at home. We have found that parents, enjoying their Bishopwyn, have become interested in the wreath and have integrated the Advent program of school and home as result of the St. Nicholas Day party.

There is a description of the "Festival of St. Nicholas" in Mary Mapes Dodge's book, *Hans Brinker or the Silver Skates* that is well worth reading aloud on this day. Therein the Dutch children sing:

> *Welcome, friend! Saint Nicholas, welcome!*
> *Welcome to this merry band!*
> *Happy children greet thee, welcome!*
> *Thou art glad'ning all the land!*

This is the traditional hymn to St. Nicholas sung in the Byzantine or Eastern Rite Church. It is an easy and very catchy tune that children will pick up quickly and will hum for days.

O WHO LOVES NICHOLAS THE SAINTLY

O who loves Ni-cho-las the saint-ly, O who serves Ni-cho-las the saint-ly, him will Ni-cho-las re-ceive, and give help in time of need. Ho-ly Fa-ther Ni-cho-las!

He who dwells in God's ho-ly man-sions is our help on the land and o-ceans. He will guard us from all ills, keep us pure and free from sin, ho-ly Fa-ther Ni-cho-las.

Holy Saint, hearken to our prayers;
Let not life drive us to despair.
All our efforts shall not wane,
Singing praises to your name,
Holy Father Nicholas.

Saint Nicholas, pray for us who love you.
O Father, humbly we beseech you.
We will always praise your name;
Your great deeds we will proclaim
Forever, forever.

The Christ Candle

An attractive Christ-Candle for the family table may be made by melting beeswax or used white candles. Take a tall, quart-sized empty can, the kind in which juice comes. Remove one end of the can. Across the open end place a pencil to which is tied a ten-inch piece of string for the wick. Pour the melted wax or beeswax into the can until full. Allow to cool. Then place in the refrigerator for an hour. When the bottom of the can is removed by a can opener the candle will slip out easily. It may be entwined with holly or other evergreens to signify the Light from the Root of Jesse and lighted at meal times.

A child may cut from old Christmas cards a Madonna and Child, a star or angel, and attach these with rubber cement to the candle. Our eight-year-old daughter decorated a delightful candle by pinning to it tiny bright metal stars, spangles and snowflakes by means of straight pins.

This candle may be blessed with the blessing found on page 84.

Mary's Candle

This day a rod came forth out of the root of Jesse;
This day Mary was conceived without any stain of sin;
This day the head of the old serpent was crushed by her, Alleluia.

Following closely is the feast of the Immaculate Conception, December 8. It is our only daughter's baptismal day, a day of great joy because (she is adopted) her rebirth in Christ is such a wonderful event in her life and in ours. On our Lady's altar our daughter arranges a single red rose in a vase and covers it with a blue lace or net to signify the Mystical Rose. On an end table in the living room, she sets up the Christ-Candle which will be lighted during Christmas. Over the candle goes a white mantle. It is usually a cape of white satin; but crepe paper fluted and gathered with ribbon will do.

Our candle, made by Brett in Germany, has a decorated crib and Christ cut into the base; but it would not be a difficult task for a grown up or even a child to paint a figure of the Infant on a short, broad candle. Our candle serves as the basis for sex instructions. "Blessed is the fruit of thy womb" becomes a reality to the littlest children who love to learn about the Baby in Mary's immaculate body. Mary is God's throne room and her part in our redemption is very great. Only He knows how often the Holy Spirit works upon children's souls as they peek under the mantle to see the Infant whose coming they await with great expectancy.

Some families have the custom of placing a candle, decorated with a small white or blue ribbon, before a statue or picture of the Blessed Virgin on the feast of her Immaculate Conception. They light the candle during meals and evening prayers. It serves as an eloquent reminder of Mary's eager expectation of the "Light of the World," and helps members of the family keep their own light of grace burning brightly as the best preparation for His coming.

As well as attending Mass on this holy day of obligation, we recite the Magnificat (text on page 46) and sing hymns at Mary's altar.

> Him whom the heavens cannot contain, the womb of one woman bore. She ruled our Ruler; she carried Him in Whom we are; she gave milk to our Bread.
>
> · St Augustine

Our Lady of Guadalupe

Who is she that comes forth like the sun, beautiful as Jerusalem?
The daughters of Sion saw her blooming among the roses, and declared
her most blessed.

It is especially fitting that we celebrate this feast of Our Lady of Guadalupe, December 12, during Advent, as it is under this title that the Virgin Mother is protectress of the unborn, as well as patroness of Mexico and the Americas. As the children are reminded of the unborn Christ Child growing under Mary's heart in the safety of her womb, they pray for her protection on all unborn children.

In addition to retelling the story of Our Lady's appearance to Blessed Juan Diego on Mount Tepeyac and the miraculous image of herself left on his tilma, the family can celebrate this feast with a meal of Mexican dishes served with homemade tortillas, the bread of the Mexican people.

Corn Tortillas

2 cups *masa harina* (prepared flour, ground of cooked corn – obtainable at most grocery stores)

½ cup water

Mix *masa harina* and water. The mixture should not be crumbly, but moist. Shape into 12 balls. To keep them from drying out, cover with plastic wrap or damp towel. Place a ball of dough between two pieces of plastic wrap and flatten in a tortilla press or with a heavy plate. Peel off the tortilla and place in a hot ungreased frying pan (cast iron works best). Cook about 1 minute on each side: the cooked tortillas should be soft. Wrap cooked tortillas in a clean towel and serve warm.

There is no comparison between fresh homemade tortillas and their mass produced counterpart; it is the difference between fresh baked bread and a store-bought loaf.

◆ ◆ ◆

For dessert, make these easy Sopapillas.

Sopapillas

Flour tortillas, cut into 4 triangles (Thick tortillas are best.)
Oil for frying
Powdered sugar, cinnamon-sugar, honey, or chocolate syrup

Pour 2" of frying oil into a deep cast iron skillet (or use a fryer) and preheat at medium-high heat for 5 minutes. Put as many tortilla triangles into the hot oil as will fit without crowding. Fry for 1 minute or until the tortilla puffs and starts to turn a golden brown. Work quickly, but carefully. Remove the tortilla from the oil with a slotted spoon or tongs and place on paper towels or brown paper bags to drain. Serve the Sopapillas warm, dusted with powdered sugar or cinnamon-sugar or dipped in honey or chocolate syrup.

MAÑANITAS A LA VIRGEN DE GUADALUPE
MORNING SONG TO THE VIRGIN

BUENOS DÍAS, PALOMA BLANCA

St. Lucy

O God, Our Savior, listen to us!
We rejoice in the feast of Your Virgin Martyr St. Lucy;
May she teach us to love you better.

The feast of St. Lucy, virgin and martyr, on December 13, marks the opening of the Christmas season in Sweden, where *Leissi Katter* or St. Lucy's Cats are a special treat. In that country the eldest daughter of the family, dressed in a white robe, girded with a red sash and crowned with a berried wreath bearing white candles, awakens her family and serves them these buns. We bake the yellow buns in the form of cats.

Leissi Katter (St. Lucy's Cats)

1 package yeast (or 2 ¼ tsp.)
1 Tb. sugar
¼ cup warm water
1 cup milk
¾ cup sugar
4 Tb. shortening
½ cup raisins

½ cup currants
2 Tb. saffron (optional)
¾ cup hot water
1 Tb. chopped citron
6 cups flour
1 tsp. salt
1 beaten egg

Add yeast and sugar to warm water. Scald and cool milk. When yeast mixture bubbles add to milk. Beat in shortening, sugar and two cups flour. Cover and let rise. Put saffron in ¾ cup hot water for one hour. Strain and add to dough only for color (optional). Combine fruits, flour and salt. Let rise again. Shape into oval buns with round heads. Add a tail it you wish. Use raisins as eyes. Brush with beaten egg and water and let rise again until it doubles its bulk. Bake in a moderate oven (350°) for 30 minutes.

❖❖❖

Advent Ember Days

In the traditional calendar of the Roman Rite, Ember Days are on Wednesday, Friday, and Saturday following the First Sunday in Lent and Pentecost Sunday, during the third full week of September, and after the Third Sunday in Advent. The Ember Days are days of fasting to sanctity the four seasons and to invoke God to bless the clergy, for whose ordination the Ember Saturdays are set apart.

Advent Ember Days receive their proper significance when children reenact the mysteries of each day's Gospel. In the Middle Ages, Holy Mother Church taught the people by mystery plays - plays about the life of Christ. Sometimes we read the Gospel and the children act it out. Other times we tell the Gospel story and let the children use their own words. One of the loveliest of such scenes was staged at Corpus Christi School where our daughter as Mary dramatized Our Lady in her home at the coming of Herod's messenger and on the subsequent journey. Scarfs, bathrobes, remnants and old lace dresses make excellent costumes.

In this connection there is a delightful hymnal *The Story of the Redemption for Children.* They love the songs. On Ember Days they sing *The Annunciation* set to the music of the Latin hymn *Creator Alme Siderum.* Another simple hymn suitable for this season and set to the same music is *The Trip to Bethlehem.*

Drop down dew,
you heavens, from above,
and let the clouds rain
the just one.
Let the earth be opened
and bud forth
the savior

THE ANNUNCIATION

1. One day while Mary knelt in prayer
She saw an angel standing there.
His glory filled teh dwelling place.
He said to her, "Hail full of Grace!"

2. Now Mary feared and bowed her head.
"Oh, do not fear," the angel said,
"For God shall send His Son to thee.
His holy Mother, thou shalt be."

3. Then Mary spoke the blessed word:
"Behold the Handmaid of the Lord.
As thou hast said, so be it done."
The Son of God became her Son.

THE TRIP TO BETHLEHEM

1. St. Joseph brushed the donkey neat,
Put Mary in the saddle seat,
Then took his staff of hickory limb,
And started off for Bethlehem.

2. They traveled on for many days
Along the ewinding dusty ways.
But no complaint was heard from them,
A trav'ling down to Bethlehem.

3. The richer folk would hurry by
In carriages all fine and high,
And proudly look away from them.
A trav'ling down to Bethlehem.

4. At last, when Joseph halted there,
The inn was full; and ev'rywhere
He heard them say, through ev'ning gloom
So sorry, sir, we have no room.

Christmas Manger

Each year our other big Advent project is the building of a manger for the entrance hall. One year the children drew the figures which Daddy glued to plywood and cut with a saw. Another year we carved Nativity figures from Ivory soap. We have also made them of cookie dough using Nativity cookie cutters. The same cookie cutters filled with plaster of paris made lovely white figures.

An important factor with children is to give them incentive to work and credit for their effort by placing the manger scene where many can admire it. This encourages further creative efforts.

About the time Advent projects are nearing completion, our children prepare banners to go with the Infant in the living room manger. They print their names on bright little cardboard banners and slip the individual banners into lollipop sticks set into plaster bases. These are placed around the crib to show that our children are among those who proclaim Christ their King. This idea may be carried out by using Children's photographs, cut out, pasted to cardboard, and made to stand around the crib.

The Advent House

Most exciting of our family customs is the Advent House with its seven sealed windows concealing symbols of Christ derived from the Old Testament. Beginning December 17th, the little House is hung against the light of a window, and the beautiful "O" antiphons of the Liturgy become our morning prayer. The little ones can hardly wait to break the seal on each Advent House window. They find within a colorful transparency depicting a symbol of Christ, such as the burning bush, they key of David, the root of Jesse, symbols which grow in richness and meaning year by year.

The antiphons, scriptural texts a few lines long, are so many jewels of inspired poetry. Each ends on the eager cry, "Come!" On December 23rd when the door of the Advent House is opened, children find little King Jesus on His Mother's knee.

"There is a climactic order in these antiphons," Father William I. McGarry, S.J., writes. "In the first, *O Sapientia*, we take a backward flight into the recesses of eternity to address Wisdom, the Word of God. In the second, *O Adonai*, we have leaped from eternity to the time of Moses and the Law of Moses (about 1400 B.C.). In the third, *O Radix Jesse*, we have come to the time when God was preparing the line of David (about 1100 BC). In the fourth, *O Oriens*, we see that the line of David is elevated so that the peoples may look on a rising star in the east, and hence in the sixth, *O Rex Gentium*, we know that He is king of all the world of man. This brings us to the evening before the vigil, and before coming to the town limits of Bethlehem, we salute Him with the last Great O, "*O Emmanuel*, God-with-us."

---

* The Advent House is no longer available at the source Mrs. McLoughlin sited. However, using the description here, a similar Advent House could be fashioned as an Advent project in the weeks preceding December 17. It is a simple house shape with seven "hinged" windows cut into it. Behind each window is glued an "O" antiphon symbol, which can be copied from the following pages or designed by a creative child. An Advent House is especially good for an older child who may have outgrown the usual ready-made Advent calendars.

O Sapientia　　　　　　　　　　**December 17**
O WISDOM
Who issued from the mouth of the Most High
Reaching from beginning to end
Ordering all things mightily yet tenderly –
COME to teach us the way of prudence.

O Adonai　　　　　　　　　　**December 18**
O LORD OF LORDS
And Leader of the house of Israel,
Who appeared to Moses in the bush's flaming fire
And gave to him the Law on Sinai —
COME to redeem us with outstretched arms.

O Radix Jesse　　　　　　　　**December 19**
O ROOT OF JESSE
A standard to the peoples
Before whom kings are mute,
To whom all nations shall appeal —
COME to deliver us; delay, please, no longer.

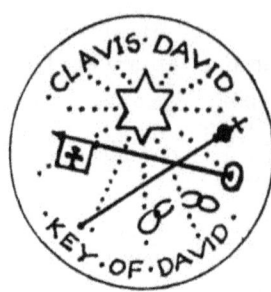

O Clavis David   December 20
O KEY OF DAVID
And Scepter of the house of Israel,
You open and no man dares shut,
You shut and no man dares open —
COME, deliver from the chains of prison
    him who sits in darkness and in the
    shadow of death.

O Oriens   December 21
O RISING DAWN
Radiance of eternal light
And Sun of Justice —
COME, enlighten those sitting in darkness
And in the shadow of death.

O Rex Gentium   December 22
O KING OF NATIONS
And their desired one,
Cornerstone who binds two into one —
COME, and save man
Whom You fashinoned from the slime of the
    earth

O Emmanuel   December 23
O EMMANUEL, God-with-us,
Our King and Lawgiver,
The Awaited of the peoples and their Savior —
COME to save us, O Lord, our God.

Tree Decorations

Making Christmas tree decorations provides one of our family's Advent projects and gives the children thoughts for meditation. A child who can draw is always happy to see his own work displayed on the tree. Children not so talented can cut out the animals of the stable, angels, and the figures of the Advent season (Isaias, John the Baptist, and Zachary) from old books, calendars or Christmas cards. These may be backed with bright colored paper to make attractive ornaments. Our children love symbols. Last year Christ, the Christmas rose, was represented by a rose (cut from wallpaper) over which they placed twelve silver stars. They also dressed tiny dolls to present Christ's ancestors and hung them on the tree. These included Jesse, David, Our Lady, St. Joseph, and Adam and Eve. Clay and paint provided a tiny apple and a serpent to give Eve real meaning and to dramatize the reason for the Redeemer's coming.

Christmas Cooking

Christ, the Bread of Angels, has been honored by special "Christmas Bread" in every European country. The French Canadian uses homemade *Pain d'Habitant*, the Czech, *Vanocka*. The Italian saves a slice from each Christmas loaf and on St Blaise Day, forty days later, soaks the hard bread in milk and eats it. Many cakes are baked in wreath-shaped pans and circles to symbolize everlasting life. Among these are the Swedish *Iulbrod*, chock full of Citron, raisins, almond; and the famous Ukrainian poppy seed cake. Most delicious of Christmas Breads are Brioche or French Christmas bread, the *Christollen* of Germany whose crisscross shape reminds us of the Child in swaddling clothes, and *Meluchrino* or Greek spice cake. The latter our children call Hidden Jesus Bread, because of the infant baked in it. Recipes for all three are from Mrs. Berger's *Cooking for Christ*, whose family like ours is large. One half of her recipe is usually sufficient for small families. Where the price of butter is prohibitive, part margarine with butter may be used.

Brioche, a very light rich bread, is best mixed on Christmas Eve so the dough can stand before it is baked. Use a very hot oven on Christmas morning to make the dough rise quickly. The crust is crisp and brown, the center soft when the dough is handled lightly.

Brioche

1 packet of yeast (or 2 ¼ tsp.)
¼ cup warm water
4 cups flour
1 tsp. salt

1 Tb. sugar
6 slightly beaten eggs
1 cup butter
½ cup milk

Mix yeast with warm water and one cups flour, Cover and set aside to rise. Mix remaining dry ingredients. Work in butter with your fingers. Add milk very slowly. (The dough should be softer than bread dough.) Mix in yeast combination and let rise one to two hours. Punch down and keep in a cold place until ready to use. Then shape into loaves. Place in two 6 x 10 loaf pans. Put in warm place until dough rises about one third more in size. Brush with beaten egg. Bake in hot oven (450°) until brown. This recipe will make two loaves.

Christollen needs plenty of room so that the shape of the Child in swaddling clothes will be surely seen in the folds of dough.

❖❖❖

Christollen

1 packet of yeast (or 2 ¼ tsp.)
1 Tb. sugar
¼ cup lukewarm water
6 cups flour
1 tsp. salt
½ tsp. nutmeg
2 cups scalded milk

1 cup shortening
1 ¼ cups sugar
2 eggs
1 cup raisins
1 cup currants
½ cup blanched almonds
½ cup chopped Citron
1 ½ tsps. lemon extract

Dissolve yeast and tsp. sugar in warm water. Cover and allow to rise. Cream shortening and sugar. Add eggs and scalded milk cooled to lukewarm. Alternate with flour sifted with salt and nutmeg. Add yeast mixture Knead until smooth. Add fruits and flavoring. Cover and let dough rise to double its bulk. Knead dough again. Shape dough into ropes about 1 ½ inches in diameter. For each large stollen make one rope three feet long and two that are two and a half feet long. Braid the dough. Bring the braid to a point at either end. Place the braid on a greased cookie sheet. Bake in a hot oven (400°) for 25 minutes or until brown. This recipe will make two large *Stollen*.

After we have received the Eucharistic Bread at Christmas Mass, we like a favorite sweet bread or spice cake which Mrs. Berger calls *Melachrino*. In Greece it is customary to hide a silver coin deep in its crust; we bake a tiny figure of the Holy Infant in the dough.

◆◆◆

Melachrino

¾ cup butter
1 2/3 cups sugar
3 eggs
¾ cup milk
1 ¾ cup flour

¼ tsp. mace
1 ¼ tsp. cinnamon
¼ tsp. ground cloves
1 ½ tsp. baking soda
¼ tsp. salt
1 ½ Tb. lemon juice

Cream butter and sugar. Beat in eggs. Add milk alternately with sifted dry ingredients. Stir in lemon juice. Pour batter into a greases 9 x 14 loaf pan. Bake in a moderate oven (350°) for 45 minutes. While the cake is still hot, ice with: 2 cups confectioner's sugar mixed with 5 or 6 Tb. water and ½ tsp. lemon juice.

Early Christians brought their bread to the altar at the offertory procession. Some of it was used for the Sacrifice; the rest received a special blessing after the Consecration, but was not changed into the Body of Christ. It was taken home as Blessed Bread.
    The mother of the family may use her powers as a member of the "royal priesthood" to which St. Peter refers in his First Epistle, sprinkle holy water over the newly made bread, and say Holy Mother Church's official blessing:

Let us pray. Lord Jesus Christ, Thou the Bread of Angels, Thou the Living Bread of Eternal Life, graciously design to bless this bread as Thou didst bless the five loaves in the desert that all who partake of it may have health of body and soul. Who livest and reignest for ever and ever. Amen.

Eating blessed bread makes such an impression upon children that no scrap of it is ever wasted "because it is God's special food."

◆◆◆

From the Italians comes a quick dessert for that busiest of days, *Vigilia di Natale*, the Vigil of Christmas It is a Cassata or Cream Tart which may be made with store sponge cake to save time.

Cassata

10-inch sponge cake
1 ½ cups cottage cheese
1 ½ cups sugar

2 tsp. almond extract
2 chopped squares of bitter chocolate

Cut cake into three layers. Beat cottage cheese, sugar, almond extract, and chocolate together. Spread this filling between layers. Chill cake in refrigerator. When cake is set, ice with:

1 egg white
1 ½ cups confectioner's sugar
1 tsp. almond extract

1/2 tsp. lemon juice
candied fruits

We go to great lengths in Christmas cooking, but there are two shortcuts which we take. One is the use of store cake in the *Cassata* above and the other the use of prepared mincemeat and, on occasion, prepared pie crust.

Mincemeat pie at Christmas was originally made in an oblong baking pan to remind us of Christ's birth in a manger, while the richness of its ingredients and spices reminds us of the gifts of the Magi. We use a standard prepared mincemeat and a standard pastry recipe for a two-crust pie. A 7x11 cake pan utilizes the dough and leaves enough scraps after the pie is trimmed for a pastry Infant Jesus. This is cut from a Nativity cookie cutter, baked separately, and placed on the manger pie. The gingerbread boy had Baby Jesus for his original model.

◆◆◆

Rice is a traditional dish in countries as widely separated as Denmark, where it is called *Risengrod*, and Spain, where *Arroz Dulce* is its name. The following recipe from Puerto Rico may be used with coconut milk; but is equally as delicious as plain American rice pudding when cow's milk is used. Prepared ahead of time, it gives a mother a chance to enjoy Christmas morning.

Arroz Dulce

½ cup raw rice
2 cups boiling water
1 ½ cups milk or coconut milk
¼ cup sugar
¼ tsp. salt

¼ cup seedless raisins
1 egg
1 tbsp. butter
1 tsp. vanilla extract

Wash rice. Put in a saucepan with the boiling water and boil 15 minutes, stirring occasionally. Drain and rinse under cold running water. Scald milk in a saucepan. Add the rice, sugar, raisins, and salt, and cook, covered, until rice is tender – about 40 minutes. Beat egg well, and add to it 2 heaping tablespoons of the rice mixture. Mix well and pour back into remaining rice mixture in the double boiler. Cook, stirring constantly for 1 minute. Add butter and stir until melted. Remove from heat. Add vanilla and mix well. Serve warm or cold.

❖❖❖

Another time-saver for a busy mother are delicious Christmas morning muffins made in a jiffy when cranberries have been prepared beforehand.

Cranberry Muffins

1 cup fresh cranberries
½ cup sugar
2 cups prepared biscuit mix

2 Tb. melted butter
2 eggs, beaten
¾ cup milk

Wash and clean the cranberries, cut them in halves, cover them with the sugar, and let stand overnight. Combine the other ingredients gently - don't worry about lumps   add the cranberries and fill well-greased muffin pans two-thirds full. Bake in a 400° oven for 20 to 25 minutes. Makes 12 two-inch muffins.

❖❖❖

For little children we feel that a birthday cake, preferably a white one with a single candle, carries out the idea of Jesus' birthday. They always enjoy singing "Happy Birthday, dear Jesus," before they cut the cake.

A family we met at a Cana conference uses traditional fruit cake as Baby Jesus' Birthday Cake. To it they add a candle for each child. Children want to give the Child a present. Christina Rosetti's poem, "What Can I Give Him?" is appealing, easy to memorize, and answers the little one who wants to give Jesus something special.

> *What can I give Him,*
> *Poor as I am?*
> *If I were a shepherd,*
> *I would bring a lamb;*
>
> *If I were a wise man,*
> *I would do my part;*
> *Yet what can I give Him?*
> *Give my heart.*

Another poem easily memorized is "Our Brother Is Born":

> *Now every child that dwells on earth,*
> *Stand up, stand up and sing:*
> *The passing night has given birth*
> *Unto the children's King.*
> *Sing sweet is the flute,*
> *Sing clear is the horn*
> *Sing joy for the children,*
> *Come Christmas morn:*
> *Little Christ Jesus*
> *Our Brother is born!*

❖❖❖

Older boys and girls will enjoy making *Christmas Lady Cookies*.

Christmas Lady Cookies

2 eggs, separated
½ cup confectioner's sugar
1 tsp. vanilla

½ cup cake flour
¼ tsp. salt

Beat egg whites until stiff; add ¼ cup sugar, beating all the while. Beat the yolks until thick and lemon colored, then beat in remaining ¼ cup sugar. Fold the white mixture into the yolks, then fold in vanilla, flour and salt. Drop on ungreased paper-lined cookie sheets and bake for 15 minutes in a slow oven (300°). When cool remove from paper and sprinkle with confectioner's sugar.

◆◆◆

English eggnog is also a tradition for Christmas.

Eggnog

4 cups milk
5 whole cloves
½ tsp. vanilla extract
1 tsp ground cinnamon
12 egg yolks

1 ½ cup sugar
4 cups cream
2 tsp. vanilla extract
½ tsp. ground nutmeg
2 ½ cups rum (optional)

Combine milk, cloves, ½ tsp. vanilla, and cinnamon in a saucepan, and heat over low heat for 5 minutes. Slowly bring to a boil. In a large bowl combine egg yolks and sugar and whisk until fluffy. Whisk hot milk slowly in small portions into egg mixture so the eggs do not curdle. Pour mixture into saucepan and cook over medium heat for 3 minutes, stirring constantly. Do not allow mixture to boil. Strain to remove cloves and let cool for an hour. Stir in cream, 2 tsp. vanilla, nutmeg, and optional rum. Refrigerate overnight before serving.

◆◆◆

Potica is a festive nut roll bread from Eastern Europe. You can make one large loaf in the traditional half-moon shape or smaller loaves to give away. This bread is very satisfying with hot chocolate after Midnight Mass.

Potica

Bread:
½ cup sugar
1 tsp. salt
¼ cup butter
1 cup hot milk
1 ½ Tb. yeast
¼ cup warm water
2 eggs
4 ½ cups flour

Filling:
4 cups ground walnuts
3 eggs
1 cup brown sugar
1/3 cup butter
1 ½ tsp. cinnamon
1 tsp. vanilla

Stir sugar, salt, and butter into hot milk. Cool to lukewarm. Dissolve yeast in warm water. Stir in milk mixture. Add eggs and half flour. Beat well. Add remaining flour and kneed until dough is stiff enough to leave sides of the bowl. Place in a lightly greased bowl, cover, and let rise 1 hour.

Filling: beat eggs slightly. Add remaining ingredients, blending well.
On a lightly floured surface, roll out dough into a large rectangle. Spread with filling. Roll up and pinch ends to seal. Place on greased baking sheet. Cover and let rise 1 hour. Brush with melted butter. Bake at 350° for 30 minutes until golden brown.

* Note: filling burns easily. Don't spread filling to edges otherwise it will leak out when rolled.

◆ ◆ ◆

As Christmas approaches, the house smells of baking, presents are wrapped and wreaths are hung. The children unveil the Christ Candle and set up their cribs. It is then that their Daddy covers the fireplace mantle with evergreens - Oregon holly when we can afford it - and centers a Madonna and Child with many vigil lights as the focal of the room. A spray of evergreen is placed across the top of every picture in the room; and a piece is wound around a huge white candle placed on the dinner table to symbolize the Light of the World for whom we have made these elaborate preparations.

Christmas

THE root of Jesse has blossomed.
The Star of Jacob has risen.
A Virgin has brought forth
the Savior!
Our God, we praise You.
— Liturgy of Christmastide

As a child in the suburbs of Boston, my Christmas Eve centered around the parish house. On the half hour groups of children with trumpet accompaniment caroled around the giant tree on the lawn or, when snow was too deep, sang on the rambling veranda. From there they went to sing in the park, at the convent, and at homes of aged parishioners. Back to the parish house, its hearth aglow, children trooped in to enjoy warm doughnuts and cider. Early in the evening high school students caroled on the same circuit. Now the parish house was bright with candles and firelight. The night was blue and so frosty cold that the trumpets cut the air. Their *Noel, Noel* traveled far and clear. In reply myriads of vigil lights, flickering against lace curtains in every house, returned a bright *Merry Christmas*. Carolers returned to the parish house for refreshments.

Half-hourly the charming custom of caroling went on. By nine o'clock the church choir arrived. When the last trolley car had left the car barns an hour later, a hush fell upon the city making peace on earth a reality. By ten-thirty parents arrived to join the singing and to free the choir for rehearsals.

I remember the breathtaking beauty of the upper church, its marble altar with golden decorations was resplendent with light. The crib gave new joy each succeeding year. With the singing of Midnight Mass our season of rejoicing began.

Afterwards families walked home together in the sharp cold nights, parents a bit ahead, boys and girls lagging behind. Everywhere vigil lights flickered in homes of the Irish immigrants who began the custom in penal days when priests were being hunted. Telling of the custom in *The Christmas Book*, Father Francis X. Weiser, S. J., writes: "The people had no churches. Priests hid in forests and caves and secretly visited the farms and homes to say Mass there during the night. When Christmas came the faithful placed burning candles in the windows so that any priest who happened to be in the vicinity would be guided to their home through the dark night. Silently he entered and was received by the devout with fervent prayers of gratitude that their home was to become a church during the Holy Night. To justify this practice in the eyes of the English soldiers, the Irish people used to explain: 'We burn the candles so that Jesus and Mary looking for a place to stay will find their way to our home.' The English authorities finding this superstition harmless did not bother to suppress it."

A Gaelic name for Christmas eve is *Oidhche na ceapairi* – Night of Cakes. I can still see the cakes through candlelight in the kitchens of my childhood. A spanking white cloth on the table set off the two-foot candle bound in evergreens and rising from a bowl of holly to symbolize the Light of the World arising from the Root of Jesse. On the polished black stove were round loaves of sweet buttery bread, flecked with currants and candied peel called Irish Christmas "cake." That bread spelled Christmas for us.

After a feast day breakfast early in the morning, our tree was stealthily brought indoors and set into its waiting stand. Balls were hung; tinsel, popcorn, and cranberries festooned to its spreading branches. Then it was time for Mass at dawn.

Various home ceremonies on Christmas Eve are perhaps the easiest of all to establish. Where children are very small they are the surest link between altar and home. If they believe in "Santa Claus," this emphasis on Christmas as the Feast of Baby Jesus and His Birthday will focus their thoughts on the Holy Child. Once Christian families succeed in giving Christmas its proper setting in the liturgical cycle, they will enjoy the feast.

In our house, Christmas begins when the children are awakened and dressed in slippers and robes. Each is given a lighted candle in honor of the lighted Christ-Candle. Family and friends gather in a darkened living room round the Nativity scene. Through the halls, the children come in a procession carrying the Infant Jesus for the living room crib, while they sing Silent Night. By the time they reach the living room door, their Daddy is ready to light the tree, then the candles at the crib and mantle, and finally the Christ Candle. There upon we all sing:

Silent Night! Holy Night!
All is calm, all is bright,
Round yon Virgin mother and Child,
Holy Infant so tender and mild.
Sleep in heavenly peace,
Sleep in heavenly peace.

Silent night, holy night!
Shepherds quake at the sight.
Glories stream from heaven afar
Heavenly hosts sing Alleluia,
Christ the Savior is born!
Christ the Savior is born.

Our eldest child then reads from the Roman Martyrology:

> In the forty-second year of the Empire of Octavian Augustus, in the Sixth Age of the world while all the earth was at peace, Jesus Christ, Eternal God, and Son of the Eternal Father, willed to consecrate the world by His gracious coming; having been conceived of the Holy Ghost, and the nine months since His conception having now passed *(all kneel)*, He was born as Man of the Virgin Mary at Bethlehem of Juda. *(Very solemnly)*:

THE BIRTHDAY ACCORDING TO THE FLESH
OF OUR LORD JESUS CHRIST.

After the reading we sing the third verse of Silent Night:

Silent night, holy night!
Son of God, love's pure light.
Radiant beams from Thy holy face
With dawn of redeeming grace,
Jesus Lord, at Thy birth
Jesus Lord, at Thy birth.

Father: Our help is in the Name of the Lord
All: Who made heaven and earth.
Father: O great mystery and wonderful sign,

All: dumb beasts saw the newborn Lord lying in a crib.

Then all present recite the Magnificat, Mary's song with which she answered her cousin Elizabeth when the latter greeted her with the words, "Blessed art thou among women, and blessed is the Fruit of thy womb."

Father: My soul magnifies the Lord,
All: and my spirit rejoices in God my Savior,
Because He has regarded the lowliness of His handmaid,
> for behold, henceforth all generations shall call me blessed,

Because He who is mighty has done great things for me,
> and holy is His Name;

And His mercy is from generation to generation
> toward those who fear Him.

He has shown might with His arm;
> He has scattered the proud in the conceit of their heart.

He has put down the mighty from their thrones
> and has exalted the lowly.

The hungry He has filled with good things
> and the rich He has sent empty away.

He has given help to Israel His servant,
> mindful of His mercy -

As He promised our fathers -
> toward Abraham and his descendants forever.

Glory be to the Father, and to the Son,
> and to the Holy Spirit.

As it was in the beginning, is now, and ever shall be,
> world without end. Amen.

The Antiphon is repeated:

All: O great mystery and wonderful sign, dumb beasts saw the new born Lord lying in a crib.

The *Magnificat* is followed by the holy Gospel according to St. Luke (2:15-20):

Father: And it came to pass, when the angels had departed from them into heaven, that the shepherds were saying to one another, "Let us go over to Bethlehem and see this thing that has come to pass, which the Lord has made known to us." So they went with haste, and they found

Mary and Joseph, and the Babe lying in the manger. And when they had seen, they understood what had been told them concerning this Child. And all who heard marveled at the good things told them by the shepherds. But Mary kept in mind all these words, pondering them in her heart. And the shepherds returned, glorifying and praising God for all that they had heard and seen, even as it was spoken to them.

All: Praise be to You, O Christ.
Father: The Word was made flesh, alleluia.
All: And dwelt among us, alleluia.
Father: O Lord, hear my prayer.
All: And let my cry come to You.

Then follows the blessing of the crib.

Father: Let us pray. We beseech Thee, Almighty God, bless this crib which we have prepared in honor of the new birth in the flesh of Thine only begotten Son, that all who devoutly see in this image the mystery of His Incarnation may be filled with the light of His Glory, who with Thee liveth and reigneth forever.
All: Amen.

Now the Mother prays the Collect from the Missal:

Mother: Let us pray. O God, who dost gladden us with the yearly expectation of our redemption, grant that we, who now joyfully receive Thine Only-begotten Son as our Redeemer, may also, without fear, behold Him coming as our Judge, Our Lord Jesus Christ, Thy Son, Who liveth and reigneth for ever and ever.
All: Amen.

In conclusion family and friends sing the *Adeste Fidelis*:

> *Adeste fidelis,*
> *Laeti triumphantes,*
> *Venite, venite in Bethlehem!*
> *Natum videte,*
> *Regem angelorum*

Venite, adoremus!
Venite, adoremus!
Venite, adoremus Dominum!

O come, all ye faithful,
Joyful and triumphant,
O come ye, o come yet to Bethlehem.
Come and behold Him,
Born the King of Angels,
   O come, let us adore Him,
   O come, let us adore Him,
   O come, let us adore Him,
Christ, our Lord.

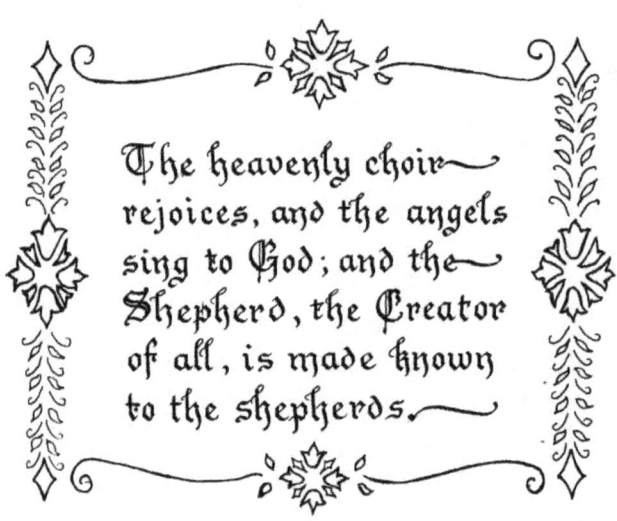

The heavenly choir rejoices, and the angels sing to God; and the Shepherd, the Creator of all, is made known to the shepherds.

Blessing of The Tree

In recent years, moreover, in a growing number of families there takes place a blessing of the Christmas tree. We like to remind our children of the part a tree played in the sins of our first parents and of the sacred wood of the Tree on which Jesus Christ, whose birthday we now celebrate, once paid the price of our redemption. Children love the story of why we use the tree. There are many versions. We tell them that the tree goes back to the Jewish Feast of Lights. It was St. Boniface who gave the balsam fir tree to the Druids in place of the oak tree, the symbol of their former idolatry. "The fir tree is the wood of peace, the sign of an endless life with its evergreen branches. It points to heaven. It will never shelter deeds of blood, but rather be filled with loving gifts and rites of kindness." When St. Ansgar preached to the Viking, he referred to the fir tree as a symbol of the faith, for it was, he said, "as high as hope, as wide as love, and bore the sign of the Cross on every bough."

The procession moves to the Christmas tree for the blessing of the tree. The following form for the blessing of the tree may be used (with a little holy water – children love to sprinkle it):

Father: This is that most worthy Tree in the midst of Paradise
All: on which Jesus by His death overcame death for all.
Father: Let the heavens be glad and the earth rejoice;
All: Let the sea and what fills it resound;
    let the plains be joyful and all that is in them!
All the trees of the forest shall exult
    before the Lord, for He comes;
for He comes to rule the earth.
    He shall rule the world with justice
and the peoples with His constancy.
    Glory be to the Father, and to the Son, and to the Holy Ghost.
As it was in the beginning, is now, and ever shall be,
    world without end. Amen.
All: This is that most worthy Tree in the midst of Paradise on which Jesus by His death overcame death for all.
Mother: God said: Let the earth bring forth vegetation: seed-bearing plants and all kinds of fruit trees that bear fruit containing their seed. And so it was. The earth brought forth vegetation, every kind of seed-bearing plant and all kinds of trees that bear fruit containing their seed. The Lord God made to grow out of the ground all kinds of trees

	pleasant to the sight and good for food, the tree of life also in the midst of the garden, and the tree of the knowledge of good and evil. And God saw that it was good.

All: Thanks be to God.

Father: O Lord, hear my prayer.

All: And let my cry come to You.

Father: Let us pray. O Lord Jesus Christ, who by dying on the tree of the Cross didst overcome the death of sin caused by our first parents' eating of the forbidden tree of paradise, grant, we beseech Thee, the abundant graces of Thy Nativity, that we may so live as to be worthy living branches of Thyself, the good and ever green Olive Tree, and in Thy strength bear the fruit of good works for eternal life. Who livest and reignest for ever and ever.

All: Amen.

In Medieval Germany, religious plays were performed to teach and entertain the peasant folk. The tree hung with the tempting apple was later moved from the stage's "Garden of Eden" into ordinary homes at Christmas, reminding families of the story of redemption. Craftsmen began blowing glass apples and eventually other shapes to decorate the Christmas tree. Thus, the glass balls which now decorate our trees find their origin in the "apple" from the story of the Fall.

Another charming custom from Germany is the *Krist Kind*. The undecorated tree is hidden in a closet or room on Christmas Eve, then brought forth on Christmas morn, having been decorated by the *Kris Kind* – the Christ Child. This symbolizes how Christ clothes and makes our souls beautiful.

Last year we served "Bread of Angels" on Christmas eve. Paper-thin wafers with Nativity scenes imprinted, these were blessed and given to each member of the family and to guests to symbolize that "all who partake of one bread are one body." With the Bread of Angels we used blessed wine. This simple fare helped us to keep the Christmas vigil fast and made it a pleasure to do so. The Bread of Angels was the gift of friends of Polish extraction.

Little children must go back to bed as midnight draws near in our house; but their brother now serves Mass. Two doors away from us the carillon of a famous church peals out the glad news of Christ's birth.

Before we leave the house, a tiny figure of the Infant is placed on the straws of the empty manger beside each child's bed. In this way the first sight to greet him or her on Christmas morning and during the season will be the Savior in swaddling clothes. We hasten to Mass in the darkness of night, reminding ourselves that we are about to celebrate the greatest act of the

Christmas feast. We go to greet that Light which now shines in the darkness; we go in the spirit of the shepherd to adore the Son of God and to offer our hearts to Him in His manger. Later during the Offertory, when bread and wine, the noblest of inanimate creatures, are offered by us and for us, we offer our children, our sorrows, our joys and ourselves on the paten, even as the divine Child offers Himself to His Father. Then we make room in our hearts for Christ, true God and
true Man, who comes to us cradled in Bread. In His coming in the Christ Mass, we undergo the divine transformation which alone makes Christmas merry. For merry in its original sense meant blessed.

Morning Prayers during The Christmas Season

Children love to pray when they realize that they are saying the same prayers as Catholics all over the world. At Christmas it is easy to introduce such prayers as a family custom. These morning prayers, with variations on special feast days, are said from Christmas eve until Candlemas. They may be used whole or in part depending on the ages of the children in one's family.

Mother: Christ is born to us!
All: Come, let us adore Him.
Father: To the King of the Ages, who is immortal, invisible, the one only God, be honor and glory forever and ever. Amen.
All: Thanks be to God.
Father: Arise, O Christ, and help us.
All: And deliver us for Your Name's sake. Lord, Have mercy on us. Christ have mercy on us. Lord, have mercy on us.
Father: Our Father, who art in heaven, *etc.*
All: But deliver us from evil.
Father: O Lord, hear my prayer.
All: And let my cry come to You.
Father: Let us pray. O Lord God Almighty, who hast brought us to the beginning of this day, preserve us in the same by Thy power that during this day we may not fall into any sin, but that all our words, thoughts and work may be directed to doing Thy holy will. Through our Lord Jesus Christ.
All: Alleluia.

Mother: This day Christ is born, this day the Savior has appeared. This day Angels are singing on earth, Archangels are rejoicing. This day the just are glad and say:
All: Glory to God in the highest, alleluia.

When children in our family are late or fussy, we sing the morning offering learned during babyhood:

"Good morning, dear God, we offer to You our thoughts, words and actions and all that we do."

This is followed by the Lord's Prayer, a Hail Mary, and an appropriate ejaculation.

Let us celebrate the festive day on which He who is the great and eternal day, came from the great and endless day of eternity into our own short day of time.
— ST. AUGUSTIN

Evening Prayers during The Christmas Season

In the evening families may again use various prayers from the liturgy of the Church.

Mother: May the Lord Almighty grant us a peaceful night and a perfect end.
All: Alleluia.
Father: Be sober, be watchful! For your adversary the devil, as a roaring lion, goes about seeking someone to devour. Resist him, steadfast in the faith.
All: Thanks be to God.
Father: Our help is in the Name of the Lord.
All: Who made heaven and earth.
Father: I confess to Almighty God,
All: to blessed Mary ever Virgin, / to blessed Michael the Archangel, to blessed John the Baptist, / to the holy apostles Peter and Paul, to all the saints, and to you my family, / that I have sinned exceedingly in thought, word, and deed: / through my fault, through my fault, through my most grievous fault. / Therefore I beseech blessed Mary ever Virgin, / blessed Michael the Archangel, blessed John the Baptist, / the holy apostles Peter and Paul, all the saints, and you my family, / to pray to the Lord our God for me.

Since children love to sing their prayers, any Christmas carol or hymn such as *Silent Night* or *Adeste Fidelis* may be sung at this time. (When children are very, very tired we simply sing a hymn and call that our evening prayer.)

Father: Protect us, Lord, while we are awake and safeguard us while we sleep, that we may keep watch with Christ and rest in peace.
Mother: Sing to the Lord a new song,
Sing to the Lord, all you lands.
All: Sing to the Lord, bless His Name;
announce His salvation, day after day.
Mother: Tell His glory among the nations
among the people His wondrous deeds.
All: For great is the Lord and highly to be praised,
awesome is He, beyond all gods.
Mother: For all the gods of the nations are things of naught,
but the Lord made the heavens.

All: Splendor and majesty go before Him,
        praise and grandeur are in His sanctuary.
Mother: Give to the Lord, you families of nations, give to the Lord glory
        and praise, give to the Lord the glory due his name!
All: Bring gifts and enter His courts,
        worship the Lord in holy attire.
Mother: Let the heavens be glad and the earth rejoice,
        let the sea and what fills it resound, let the plains be joyful and all that
        is in them!
All: Then shall all the trees of the forest exult
        before the Lord, for He comes,
        for He comes to rule the earth.
Mother: He shall rule the world with justice
        and the peoples with His constancy.
All: Protect us, Lord, while we are awake and safeguard us while we
        sleep, that we may keep watch with Christ and rest in peace.
Father: O Lord, hear my prayer.
All: And let my cry come to You.

[Here are added the prayers for special feasts.]

Father: Let us pray. Visit this home, we beseech Thee, O Lord, and drive
        far from it all snares of the enemy. Let Thy holy Angels dwell herein
        to keep us in peace, and let Thy blessing be always upon us. Through
        Jesus Christ Our Lord.
All: Alleluia.
Father: May the blessing of Almighty God, Father, Son, and Holy Spirit,
keep us forever.
All: Alleluia.

Prayers in our house are said at the crib during Christmas. It might be well for parents to meditate on the words of Abbott Marmion: "When we would penetrate into the sanctuaries of God's secrets, He says to us: 'This is my beloved Son, hear ye Him.' This is the solution of all: Jesus stretching out His little arms to us in the crib is God. As we gaze on Jesus, we have no difficulty in understanding that God is love."

   Parents should avoid buying the ugly representations of the Babe of Bethlehem which flood the market at this time of year. It is better to carve a Madonna and Child from soap or to encourage children to draw and cut out their own Nativity figures. A Hummel infant in a wooden manger is more effective than a set of cheap figures. If your children are too small to have a delicate statue under their tiny hands, some lovely Nativity scenes of folded cardboard are usually available at a religious goods store or online.

Rise, shepherds, though the night is deep,
Rise from your slumber's dreaming!
Jesus, the shepherd, watch does keep,
In love all men redeeming!
Hasten to Mary, and look for her Child,
Come, shepherds, and greet our Savior mild!

—Austrian Shepherd's Song

Caroling

When Advent hymns have been sung until December 24, there is a delightful freshness to Christmas carols. Among our favorites are *Christ was Born on Christmas Day* and *Little Jesus, Hang Your Head, You Has Got a Manger Bed.* There are many American carols, among them Holland's *There's a Song in the Air*, which stresses the kinship of Christ. *The Shepherds*, from *The Story of the Redemption for Children* published by the Gregorian Institute of America, is one which children learn easily.

THE SHEPHERDS

O COME ALL YE FAITHFUL

HARK! THE HERALD ANGELS SING

LO, HOW A ROSE E'ER BLOOMING

IN DEEPEST WINTER

Clotilde Zehnder Peter Kwasniewski

In deepest winter, earth bowed down
  With frozen heart and mind of ice
  While darkness wrapped it all around
  And hid the life within.

Yet through the darkness of that night
  Amid the frozen, weeping trees
  A star reached out to touch the place
  Wherein a baby lay.

This child lies with ox and cow,
  Yet kings come far, and heavens bend
  To sinful earth to worship him
  Who lies in golden light.

Feasts During the Christmas Season

St. Stephen, December 26

Leading the great saints who radiate from the Christ-Child is St. Stephen, First of the martyrs, he was stoned by the Jews because he courageously proclaimed that Jesus was Messiah. His name signifies the crowned. In a day like ours, when hatred of enemies floods the minds of Children, the soldier-saint Stephen, who loved his enemies, is an excellent model for them and for us.

On St. Stephen's Day our night prayers at the crib are varied in this fashion from those on pages 53-54:

Father: Christ, the New-born, today crowned blessed Stephen.
All: Come, let us adore Him.
Mother: Stephen, full of grace and power, was working great wonders and signs among the people.
All: Thanks be to God.

Father: You crowned him with glory and honor, O Lord.
All: You have given him rule over the works of Your hands.

Father: Let us pray. Grant, O Lord, we beseech Thee, that we may imitate him whose memory we celebrate, so as to learn to love even our enemies; because we now solemnize his martyrdom who knew how to pray even for his persecutors to our Lord Jesus Christ Thy Son, who liveth and reigneth forever.
All: Alleluia.

St. John, Apostle and Evangelist, December 27

When our children were little, we celebrated the feast of St. John very simply. After blessing wine with holy water and the Sign of the Cross, we made a punch, adding water and sugar, and poured it into our best goblets. Then at the supper table Daddy would begin the toast, touching his goblet to mine, and say: "I drink you the love of St. John." In turn I touched the goblets of each of the children. They followed suit and would "drink you the love of St. John." It is a delightful custom and one they cherish.

Its memory comes back to them many times. Not infrequently when they are given a special drink – even in warm weather – they say: "Today is such a saint's feast! Let's drink to his love." And the clinking of glasses begins as they toast the patron of the day.

Now that they are older we have a more solemn blessing in memory of St. John, who remained unharmed by a cup of poisoned wine after he had blessed it with the Sign of the Cross. Whenever a priest of the family is home, the 22nd Psalm is read, followed by the Lord's Prayer and a series of versicles. Then the official prayers for the Blessing of Wine are recited. Otherwise the following blessing from the Ritual is read at the dinner table:

Father: Lord Jesus Christ, Thou didst call Thyself the vine and Thy holy Apostles the branches; and out of all those who love Thee, Thou didst desire to make a good vineyard. Bless this wine and pour into it the might of Thy benediction so that everyone who drinks or takes of it, may through the intercession of Thy beloved disciple, the holy

Apostle and Evangelist John, be freed from every disease or attack of illness and obtain health of body and soul. Who livest and reignest forever.

All: Amen.

A toast to the love of St. John is then pledged by all the family.

St. John's Wine

2 cups wine
2 inches cinamon
¼ tsp. nutmeg

2 whole cloves
1 cardamon seed

Boil the spices in the wine for about five minutes. Strain the wine. Serve hot.

◆◆◆

Holy Innocents, December 28

Holy Innocents or "Childermas Day" is celebrated on December 28. The Gospel tells the story simply. "Herod slew all the boys in Bethlehem who were two years old or under." He had intended to include the Son of God among the murdered babies. To honor these young martyrs the Church wears red today. In Mass she hushes her joyous *Gloria in Excelsis* and the *Alleluias*.

And yet there is joy in her services. Children sing with the choirs in the great cathedrals; and in ancient times other functions were given to them – hence the name "Childermas" or Children's Mass.

The feast of the Holy Innocents is an excellent time for parents to inaugurate the custom of blessing their children. From the Ritual comes the form which we use on solemn occasions, such as First Communion. But all parents need to do is to sign a cross on the child's forehead with the right thumb dipped in holy water and say: "May God bless you, and may He be the Guardian of your heart and mind – the Father, Son, and Holy Spirit. Amen."

As I go from bed to bed at night, I just make the Sign of the Cross with my hand over each child while saying: "May God the Father, Son, and Holy Spirit keep you safe this night."

The custom of blessing children is easiest to establish with a baby or toddler and it grows with them. For older children the realization that parental blessings are as old as the human race can be established from reading the Old Testament. Abraham, Isaac, and Jacob blessed their children. Before his

journey Tobias blessed his son with the words: "May you have a good journey, and God be with you on your way, and His angels accompany you." I have seen a newly ordained priest kneel for his parents' blessing and then give them his first blessing. It is easy for a child who receives his father's or mother's blessing to see them as God's representatives. Encouraging parental blessings, St. Ambrose says: "You may not be rich; you may be unable to bequeath great possessions to
your children; but one thing you can give them – the heritage of your blessing. And it is better to be blessed than to be rich."

We commemorate the spilling of the blood of the Holy Innocents by using a cherry or strawberry sauce, the kind you buy or preserve, poured over a vanilla pudding or ice cream. A traditional recipe for the day, given in *Cooking for Christ*, is:

Blanc Mange

3 cups milk
¼ cup cornstarch
4 Tb. sugar

1 pinch salt
1 beaten egg
1 tsp. almond flavoring

Scald 2 ¼ cups of milk. Mix ¾ cup of cold milk, cornstarch, two tablespoons of sugar and salt. Add slowly to the hot milk. Cool until thick (about five minutes). Add egg and rest of sugar. Finish cooking for a minute or two. Flavor with almond. Mold.

* Mrs. Berger adds that it is a sure trick to add two or three tablespoons of the hot cornstarch mixture to the egg before stirring it into the pudding to prevent curdling. Rennet, junket, or a Bavarian cream may be used in place of Blanc Mange.

◆◆◆

Prayers for Childermas include a versicle and the Collect from the Mass in addition to those on pages 53-54.

Father: Enraged, Herod put to death many male children
All: In Bethlehem of Juda, the City of David.
Father: Let us pray. O God, whose praise the martyred Innocents this day proclaimed not by speaking but by dying, put to death all vices within

us, that Thy faith which our tongues profess, our lives also by their actions may declare.

All: Amen.

LULLY, LULLAY (COVENTRY CAROL)

Feast of the Holy Family, December 30

The Church has placed during Christmastide the Feast of the Holy Family as a day for the restoration of the true spirit of family life. Americans and Canadians should be rightly proud of this feast. It is North American in origin, founded in Montreal in 1663. The Mass and Office of the day give Christian parents an opportunity to pray that their family life may be sanctified by the Holy Spirit. Family life becomes sanctified when parents carry out St. John Chrysostom's plea to make each home a family church. This idea may seem far-fetched. Yet Christians fulfill the sacrament of Matrimony in their homes. Penance and Holy Eucharist are administered in the home in times of sickness, as is the sacrament of Anointing of the Sick. In danger of death, a newborn baby may receive Baptism at home.

It is in today's Reading that families will find norms for shaping Christ-like lives. "Brethren, put on therefore, as God's chosen ones, holy and beloved, a heart of mercy, kindness, humility, meekness, patience. Bear with one another and forgive one another, if anyone has a grievance against any other; even as the Lord has forgiven you, so also do you forgive. But above all these things have charity, which is the bond of perfection. And may the peace of Christ dwell in you abundantly; in all wisdom teach and admonish one another by psalms, hymns, and spiritual songs, singing in your hearts to God by his grace. Whatever you do in word or in work, do all in the name of the Lord Jesus, giving thanks to God the Father through Him."

On this Feast of the Holy Family, we vary the usual Christmastide prayers by using the following hymn. The sentiments expressed make it peculiarly appropriate as a Christian family song.

UBI CARITAS ET AMOR

Repeat first line

Where charity and love are, God is there.
Christ's love has gathered us into one.
Let us rejoice in Him and be glad.
Let us fear, and let us love the living God.
And may we love each other with a sincere heart.

Solemnity of Mary, Mother of God

The Church sanctifies the first day of the New Year in a most special manner; all Catholics are to gather around the altar to dedicate this new segment of time to God, the Author of time. Since it is the octave day of Christmas and since Mary stands at the beginning of the new age of redemption, New Year's Day is also the Solemnity of Mary, Mother of God. The liturgy of the Church would have us reflect upon and respond spiritually to these three magnificent themes today: Mary, Christmas, New Year's Day.

True beauty is yours O Mary! The stain of original sin has never marred you

New Year's is a day of hospitality among many people, especially the French. In England it was a day set aside for godparents; and godcakes are still given to children on this day in many places. It should be easy to keep New Year's Day as a feast on which we honor godparents and repay them for the responsibility they have assumed toward our children.

An idea is to hold open house and let the children's godparents drop in when they please. Have ready beer or ale for grown-ups, and a children's punch. Perhaps you might serve beer which has been blessed and pretzels for grown-ups, punch plus initial cookies for children. Pretzels, incidentally, were originally made in the shape of praying hands by medieval monks who gave them to children visitors.

Blessing for Beer

This prayer attributes the power of brewing to God and asks Him to make the beverage beneficial to man. The father sprinkles beer with holy water and prays:

Bless, O Lord, this created thing, beer, which by Thy power has been made from kernels of grain. May it be a healthful beverage for men; and grant that by invoking Thy holy Name all who drink thereof may find it a help for the body and protection for the soul Through Christ our Lord. Amen.

❖ ❖ ❖

Children's Punch

1 quart cranberry juice
1 can frozen lemonade concentrate

1 can frozen orange juice concentrate
1 can pineapple juice
Ginger ale as needed

Combine cranberry juice, orange juice, and lemonade concentrate with the pineapple juice and enough ginger ale to make desired strength. Pour over ice in a punch bowl and garish with maraschino cherries and pieces of pineapple.

❖❖❖

Initial Cookies

2/3 cup butter or margarine
1 cup sugar
2 yolks or 2 whole eggs

4 cups pastry flour
½ tsp. almond flavoring

Cream butter and sugar, add eggs and blend together until smooth. Add almond flavoring and flour. Chill for 1 hour in a long roll. Then form into the initials of the godparents visiting for the day. Allow to stand 2 or 3 hours on a cookie sheet to dry the surface. Then brush with egg white mixed with a tablespoon of milk; and sprinkle with chopped almond and sugar. Bake in a moderate oven for about 15 minutes. These cookies are like almond pretzels.

❖❖❖

Bring out their christening robes, if you have saved them. Reminisce about each child's baptismal day, which is his or her rebirth in Christ. With godparents and family gathered in the living room, light the children's baptismal candles, or light a holy candle for each child. When the candles are ready, the father presents one to each child and prays as the Church did at baptism:

Receive this burning light, and safeguard your baptism by a blameless life. Keep the Commandments of God, that when our Lord shall come to claim His own, you may be worthy to greet Him, with all the saints in the heavenly court, and live forever. Amen.

Grown-ups and children repeat together their baptismal vows:

I (name) promise to renounce the devil and all his works and allurement.

Mother: The grace of God our Savior has appeared to all men, instructing us, in order that by rejecting ungodliness and worldly lusts, we may live temperately and justly and piously in this world.

Then follows a Christmas song and the prayer of the day.

The Word was made flesh, al-le-lu-ia, al-le-lu-ia.
And dwelt a-mong us, al-le-lu-ia, al-le-lu-ia.
Glo-ry be to the Fath-er and to the Son and to the Ho-ly Ghost.
(Repeat first two lines)

Father: By reason of His very great love
All: Wherewith He has loved us, God sent His Son in the likeness of sinful flesh, alleluia.
Father: Let us pray. O God, by the fruitful Virginity of the Blessed Mary Thou hast given to mankind the rewards of eternal salvation; grant, we beseech Thee, that we may benefit through the intercession of her by whom we received the Author of Life, our Lord Jesus Christ.
All: Amen.

A New Year's Day ceremony takes only a few minutes, but leaves a memory that lasts a lifetime and builds a sense of security in children. It also focuses their attention on the wonderful gift of Baptism.

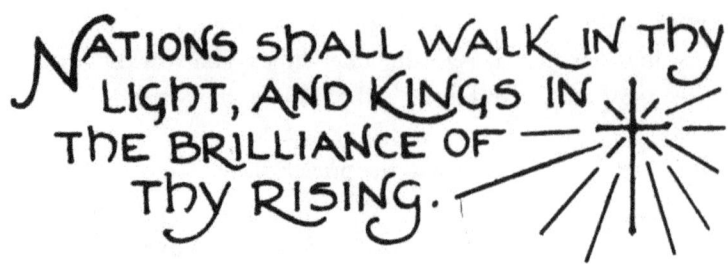

Epiphany

Like so many of our family customs, the celebration of the King's Feast, or Epiphany, began when our children were toddlers. They put their shoes outside the door for gifts from the Kings, and a few almond cookies with a small toy were all they received. In their visit the Wise Men left a tiny gold paper crown on each Christ-Child figure, and raised the family manger to a throne draped in red corduroy and gold paper. (Red crepe paper is equally effective). At the Nativity scene they left figures of the Magi and their retinue.

I used to make paper crowns of gold so each of our children could be a King. Then, using bright pieces of fabric, I would hem both ends and draw a contrasting wide ribbon through one. This gathered the material into a cape for the King. The children chose their names – Caspar, Baltassar, Melchior. Their day was spent journeying to Bethlehem on rocking-horse or tiny sawhorse camels. At supper we served a simple cake with white frosting topped by a crown of gumdrops. Three pieces of the cake were given away in honor of the Wise Men. It was always a job to keep the crown from losing its "jewels" before it was served. After supper each child was tossed to the ceiling three times, in honor of each of the Magi; then the ritual began.

With three Kings in procession we blessed the house with holy water and marked the doors with blessed chalk. We put 19 + C + M + B + 56, using the initials of the Magi and the year, so that our coming and going would be in search of the Truth. The baby would be rocked to sleep with *We Three Kings of Orient Are*, while the others cuddled up to hear carols. We lived in a Spanish neighborhood and were not alone in celebrating "The King's Feast." Although small, the children had fulfilled its chief purpose – to honor Christ as King.

Epiphany means the revelation of the Messiah's coming to the Gentiles whom the Magi represent. It is one of the five days of the year called "a day most holy" in the Canon of the Mass. In Spain, Portugal, Central and South America, the feast is kept with almost as much solemnity as Christmas. Now that our children are older - the oldest ten - the blessing of our apartment is sometimes given by a priest. Using water blessed on the eve of Epiphany, he reads a Christmas antiphon, the Magnificat, two prayers, and the final blessing.

In the absence of a priest the family gathers around the crib with lighted candles and recites or sings:

All: A Child is born in Bethlehem, alleluia!
Full joyous sings Jerusalem, alleluia, alleluia.
From Orient, behold the star, alleluia,
And holy kings come from afar, alleluia, alleluia,

The father reads the Gospel for the Feast of the Epiphany, St. Matthew 2:1-12.

All: From the East came the magi to Bethlehem to adore the Lord; and opening their treasures, they offered costly gifts: gold to the Great King, incense to the True God, and myrrh in symbol of His burial, alleluia!

While the father sprinkles the rooms of the house with Epiphany water obtained from the church or with ordinary holy water, the mother and children recite the canticle of the Blessed Mary, the Magnificat (found on page 46). Then follow the prayers:

All: From the East came the Magi to Bethlehem to adore the Lord; and opening their treasures, they offered costly gifts: gold to the Great King, incense to the True God, and myrrh in symbol of His burial, alleluia!
Father: Many shall come from Saba.
All: Bearing gold and incense.
Father: O Lord, hear my prayer.
All: And let my cry come unto Thee.
Father: Let us pray. O God, who by the guidance of a star didst this day reveal Thy Only-Begotten Son to the Gentiles, grant that we who know Thee by faith may be brought to the contemplation of the heavenly majesty. Through the same Jesus Christ.
All: Amen.
All: Be enlightened and shine forth, O Jerusalem, for thy light is come and upon thee is risen the glory of the Lord, Jesus Christ, born of the Virgin Mary.

Father: Nations shall walk in thy light, and kings in the brilliance of thy rising.
All: And the glory of the Lord is risen upon thee.
Father: Let us pray. O Lord, Almighty God, bless this house that it may become a shelter of health, chastity, self-conquest, humility, goodness, mildness, obedience to the Commandments, and thanksgiving to God, Father, Son, and Holy Spirit. Upon this house and those who dwell herein may Thy blessing remain forever. Through Christ our Lord.
All: Amen.

With blessed chalk the lintels above the door are marked with the initials of the three kings and with crosses. We use the following form:

Father: Let us pray. O Lord God, through the power of the priest Thou didst bless this creature chalk to make it helpful to man. Grant that we who use it with faith and inscribe with it the names of Thy saints Caspar, Melchior, and Balthasar upon the entrance of our homes, may through their merits and petition enjoy physical health and spiritual protection. Through Christ our Lord.
All: Amen

The father then writes the initials of the names of the Magi separated by crosses and the year above the door in this manner;

$$20 + C + M + B + \text{(year, last two digits)}$$

In conclusion the following hymn is sung or prayed:

> The star of Jacob leadeth them, alleluia!
> From Saba to blest Bethlehem, alleluia, alleluia.
> Gold, myrrh, and incense pure they bring, alleluia.
> To Mary's Child, God, Man and King, alleluia, alleluia!

This home service may also be used the evening before Epiphany or any day during the Octave.

Sometimes a mother will say, "Our children are too big for processions - John is eleven." Boys of eleven or any age love cake. Forget the processions if your children are older, and teach them a joyful wholesome use of food, as the

Church intends, by celebrating feast days. For King's Day let a boy or girl bake a cake with prepared mixes and then build a gumdrop crown on it. Better still, fill the house with a feeling of the Epiphany by baking a traditional cake with a bean in it, letting whoever receives the bean be King for the day.

Twelfth Night Cake

1 cup butter or margarine	1/3 tsp. salt
2 2/3 cups sugar	1 ½ cups milk
5 ½ cups flour	2 tsp. vanilla
5 tsp. baking powder	6 beaten egg whites

Cream shortening and sugar. Add milk alternately with sifted dry ingredients. Fold in beaten egg whites. Add vanilla. Bake in three 9 inch greased layer tins in a moderate oven (375) for about 30 minutes. Frost and top the cake with a crown of gumdrops.

◆◆◆

Epiphany Gift

An inexpensive gift for children is candied fruit peel. Its jeweled crustiness makes it ideal for Epiphany. Somehow the commercial producers have a way of making all peel taste the same. Peel may be wrapped in gold paper as gifts for a children's Epiphany party.

>Remove peel from oranges, grapefruit, or lemons - as much as you wish to candy. Be sure that white inner rind stays on peel. Slice it into ¼ inch wide strips, as long and uniform as possible. Place in a saucepan, cover with cold water, bring to a boil, and pour off liquid. Repeat process five more times.
>
>After sixth boiling, cover peel with cold water, boil peel until tender; then pour off water. Measure peel in a measuring pitcher, add an equal quantity of sugar, put both back into saucepan. Add barely enough water to be seen through the peel, bring water to a boil. Reduce heat and simmer until syrup is thick. This will take several hours.
>
>Place a wire cake cooler in a large flat roasting pan and spread peel over wire. When it is well drained and cold, roll the peel in granulated sugar and let it stand overnight. It may be necessary to

roll peel in sugar again the second day. Place in airtight container until ready for use or roll in gold paper as a gift.

❖❖❖

Epiphany Evening Prayers

For the families that do not have an Epiphany home service, the following evening prayers are appropriate.

Father: Christ has appeared among us.
All: Come, let us adore Him.
Mother: The precious gifts which the Magi brought to the Lord this day are threefold, and they are signs of divine mysteries. By the gold the power of the King is signified, by frankincense His great priesthood, by myrrh the burial of the Lord.
All: The Magi worshipped the Author of our salvation in the crib, and of their treasures they brought to Him gifts of mystic nature.
Youngest Child: Glory be to the Father and to the Son and to the Holy Spirit.
All: As it was in the beginning, is now and ever shall be, world without end. Amen.
Father: Let us pray. O God, by the leading of a star Thou didst manifest Thine only begotten Son to the Gentiles on this day; mercifully grant that we who know Thee by faith, may be brought to contemplate the beauty of Thy majesty. Through the same Jesus Christ Thy Son.
All: Alleluia.

A LIGHT TO THE GENTILES

ANGELS FROM THE REALMS OF GLORY

1. Angels from the realms of glory,
Wing your flight o'er all the earth;
Ye who sang creation's story,
Now proclaim Messiah's birth:
Come and worship, come and worship,
Worship Christ, the newborn King.

2. Shepherds, in the fields abiding,
Watching o'er your flocks by night,
God with man is now residing,
Yonder shines the infant light:
Come and worship, come and worship,
Worship Christ, the newborn King.

3. Sages, leave your contemplations,
Brighter visions beam afar;
Seek the great Desire of nations,
Ye have seen his natal star:
Come and worship, come and worship,
Worship Christ, the newborn King.

4. Though an infant now we view him,
He shall fill his Father's throne,
Gather all the nations to him;
Every knee shall then bow down:
Come and worship, come and worship,
Worship Christ, the newborn King.

5. All creation, join in praising
God, the Father, Spirit, Son,
Evermore your voices raising,
To the eternal Three in one:
Come and worship, come and worship,
Worship Christ, the newborn King.

AS WITH GLADNESS MEN OF OLD

EARTH HAS MANY A NOBLE CITY

1. Earth has many a noble city; Beth-l'hem, thou dost all excel; Out of thee the Lord from heaven Came to rule his Israel.
2. Fairer than the sun at morning Was the star that told his birth, To the world its God announcing Seen in fleshly form on earth.
3. Eastern sages at his cradle Make oblations rich and rare; See them give, in deep devotion Gold and frankincense and myrrh.
4. Sacred gifts of mystic meaning: Incense doth their God disclose; Gold the King of kings proclaimeth; Myrrh his sepulcher foreshows.
5. Jesus, whom the Gentiles worshiped At thy glad epiphany, Unto thee, with God the Father And the Spirit, glory be.

SONGS OF THANKFULNESS AND PRAISE

The following hymn serves well as a conclusion. Additional verses may be composed by members of the family.

THE WISE MEN

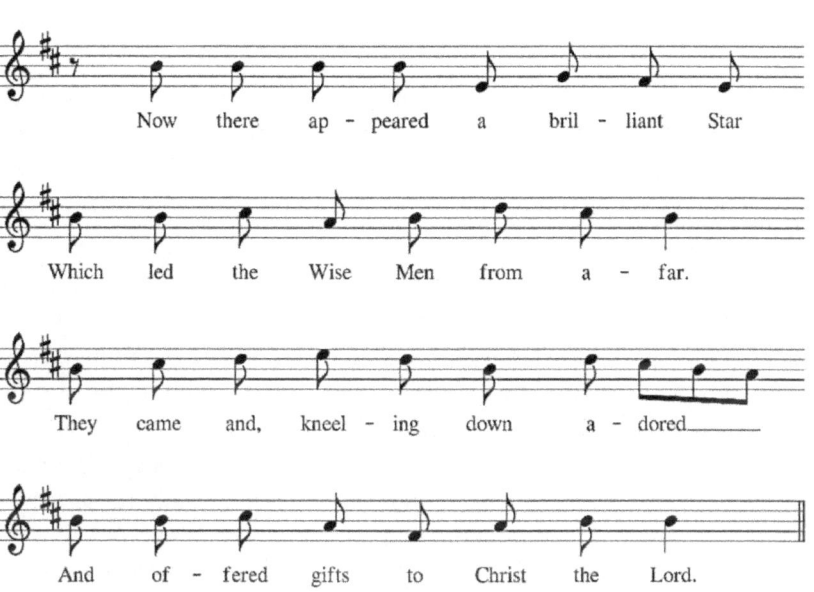

Feasts of The Epiphany Season

January 19 and 21

On the feast of St. Canute the Fourth, the Danes honor a great king and martyr. At Christmas a cake baked in the form of a boar is brought to the dining room table, but it is not eaten until St. Canute's Day, January 19, when their Christmas season ends.

We use a somewhat similar custom on the feast of St. Agnes, two days later. A cake is baked on her feast in a lamb mold. It is frosted white and made woolly with coconut shreds. Raisins serve for the eyes, a half cherry for the mouth. The cake has a two-fold meaning. It commemorates St. Agnes' name which means lamb or victim in Latin, and pure in Greek. It also reminds our children of the custom of placing two lambs on the altar of the Basilica where her relics lie. The animals are blessed by the abbot and sent to a Cloister where they are reared. From their wool come the palliums sent by the Pope to archbishops who wear them on their shoulders as symbols of the sheep carried by the Good Shepherd.

St. Agnes is a wonderful saint for teenagers because she remained innocent amid pagan corruption and died at thirteen rather than sully herself. Rome still keeps marked the path she trod to martyrdom.

A suitable prayer for today (in addition to those on page 53) is from the hymn by Adam of St. Victor:

Father: Let us gain courage for our own battle by honoring the martyrdom of the glorious virgin Agnes. St. Agnes, vessel of honor, flower of unfading fragrance, beloved of the choirs of Angels, you are an example to the worth of virtue and chastity. O you who wear a Martyr's palm and a Virgin's wreath, pray for us that, though unworthy of a special crown, we may have our names written in the list of Saints.

All: Alleluia.

St. Brigid's Day, February 1

The Irish love to sing at their work. Ancient Gaelic songs for all kinds of work may still be heard at the annual *Feis* ("fesh" or festival) in big cities. There are songs for milking and for gathering honey, spinning songs and carding songs. Their rhythm always follows the motions of the body. So it isn't surprising when Maura Laverty in her *Cookbook* recommends any song in waltz time for the kneading of *Harm Bruck*, a traditional Irish bread for St. Brigid's Day on February 1. It is a wholesome golden loaf sparkling with a shining sugar glaze.

Barm Brack

4 cups flour	1 cup milk (tepid)
1 tsp. cinnamon	1 beaten egg
1 Tb. yeast	¾ cup raisins
4 Tb. butter	½ cup currants
6 Tb. sugar	4 Tb. chopped peel

Warm milk until it is lukewarm. Melt butter in it. Cream yeast with 1 tablespoon of sugar and add ½ tepid milk mixture. Add beaten egg. Sift cinnamon with flour into a bowl. Make a well in the center and pour the yeast mixture into it. Sprinkle with flour and leave in a warm place until yeast forms a honey-comb. Mix to a dough with remainder of the milk. Turn onto a floured board. Knead into mixture 5 tablespoons of sugar, ¾ cup of raisins, ¼ cup of currants, and 4 tablespoons of chopped peel.

The fineness of texture of yeast bread depends upon thorough kneading. It is a one, two, three movement, and to do it properly, you must get rhythm into it. Miss Laverty writes: "I find it helps me to sing 'Red, red roses' as I knead." After dough is smooth and elastic, put the bread into a bowl, brush it with butter, cover, and leave in a warm place until doubled in bulk. Knead again, put into greased pans, brush with butter, and cover until it rises to the top of the pans (about 1 hour). Bake 40 minutes at 450°. A few minutes before the cooking is finished, take the Brack from the oven, brush with egg white, sprinkle with fine sugar, and return to the oven for a minute or two.

Feast of The Presentation

The feast of the Presentation of Our Lord in the Temple closes the forty days of the Christmas season. The day, February 2, is also called the feast of Candlemas. On this day each member of the family should receive his or her own blessed candle to be lighted on birthdays, baptismal anniversaries, first Holy Communion, and in sickness. This is another appropriate occasion to invite friends to a home ceremony.

The family, who with lighted candles goes in spirit to the Temple with our Lady, will learn a wonderful lesson of her humility. When Mary went to offer her first-born Son, Joseph carried the offering of the poor: two turtle-doves, symbols of purity and fidelity. According to Jewish law, one would be offered as a holocaust and the other for a sin offering. The Book of Leviticus reads: *The priest shall make atonement for her sin, and thus she will be made clean.* Actually Mary, the God-bearer, was not subject to such a rite – no "purification" was necessary after a virginal giving birth to Christ. Nevertheless, in her humility she observed the Law.

As the Holy Family enter the Temple, the aged Simeon and Anna, called by the Holy Spirit, wait to see the Child. It had been promised to Simeon that he would not die until he had seen the Savior. Mary, the living "Ark of the Covenant," guided by the same Spirit, welcomes the saintly old man and puts the Salvation of the World into his arms. "Now," he says, "Thou dost dismiss Thy servant in peace, O Lord, because mine eyes have seen Thy salvation which Thou hast prepared to enlighten the Gentiles, and the glory of Thy people Israel."

The blessing of candles, which takes place on this feast, is one of the three principal popular blessings conferred by the Church. Ashes and palms are the other two. The father of a family begins the home ceremony by gathering the family in candlelight around the crib for a last time.

Father: Lord Jesus Christ, the true Light that enlightens every man who comes into the world, pour forth Thy blessing upon these candles;

sanctify them by the light of Thy grace and mercifully grant that as candles by their visible light scatter the darkness of night, so too our hearts, burning with invisible fire, may be freed from all blindness of sin. With the eyes of our soul purified by Thy Light, may we discern those things that are pleasing to Thee and helpful to us, so that having finished the darksome journey of this life, we may come to never-fading joys through Thee, O Jesus Christ, Savior of the world. In perfect Trinity Thou livest and reignest God forever.

All: Alleluia.

Christmas evening prayers follow the blessing (page 53).

With the family and friends we usually have a candlelight procession from the dining room through the halls to the living room. There a Simeon of ten in a borrowed white Jewish prayer cap awaits Mary with her doll, wrapped in swaddling clothes to symbolize Baby Jesus, and a young Joseph carrying a cage with two pigeons made from modeling clay. In candlelight Simeon takes the child and prays his canticle. Then he blesses Joseph and Mary and adds: "Behold, this Child is destined for the fall and for the rise of many in Israel, and for a sign that shall be contradicted. And thy own soul a sword shall pierce, that the thoughts of many hearts may be revealed."

Then the Antiphon, "It had been revealed to Simeon by the Holy Spirit, that he should not see death before he had seen the Christ of the Lord," is sung or said in unison. A family could easily make its own prayer to the Queen of Heaven, asking that the graces of Forty days remain with them for the year.

There is a prayer by Abbot Gueranger which we like for Candlemas:

O Blessed Mother, the sword is already in your heart. You foreknow the future of the fruit of your womb. May our fidelity in following him through the coming mysteries of His public life bring some alleviation to the sorrows of your maternal heart.

O magnum
mysterium
et admirabile
sacramentum, ut
animalia viderent
Dominum natum
jacentem in
praesepio:
Beata Virgo
cujus viscera
meruerunt portare
Dominum Christum.

Resources

1. Advent wreaths, candles, Advent calendars, Jesse tree ornaments, "O" Antiphons, and more:
   - Dumb Ox Publications: dumb-ox.com
   - Autom: autom.com
   - Leaflet Missal: leafletonline.com
   - The Catholic Company: catholiccompany.com
   - Etsy: etsy.com

2. For beeswax candle rolling and dipping kits and supplies, visit the following websites:
   - Better Bee: betterbee.com
   - Glory Bee: glorybee.com
   - Etsy: etsy.com
   - HearthSong: hearthsong.com
   - Holy Heroes and Illuminated Ink have inexpensive kits that contains colored beeswax sheets for making your own Advent candles.
     - holyheroes.com
     - illuminatedink.com

3. Catholic Icing is a website that has affordable crafts and activities to print for saints' feast days, Advent, Christmas, and more.
   Visit catholicicing.com

4. Catholic Inspired has a set of lovely printable Jesse Tree ornaments to color and cut out. The website also offers many activities and coloring sheets for other Advent feast days.
   Visit catholicinspired.com

5. St. Nicholas Center is an excellent resource for celebrating the feast. It includes stories, history, music, games, and more.
   Visit stnicholascenter.org

6. Saints, Feasts, Family is a website that has biographies, prayers, traditions, songs, books, crafts, and recipes for saints throughout the year.
   Visit saintsfeastsfamily.com

7. *A Continual Feast,* by Evelyn Vitz
   This cook book is filled with recipes and traditions for the liturgical calendar.

8. *Drinking with St. Nick – Christmas Cocktails for Sinners and Saints,* by Michael P. Foley

9. Advent and Christmas Artwork:
   - National Gallery of Art: shop.nga.gov
   - The Metropolitan Museum Store: store.metmuseum.org
   - Etsy: etsy.com
   - Zazzle: zazzle.com

Book List

Picture Books

- *The Miracle of St. Nicholas* – Gloria Whelan
- *The Legend of St. Nicholas* – Demi
- *The Baker's Dozen: A Saint Nicholas Tale* – Aaron Shepard
- *St. Nicholas and the Nine Gold Coins* – Jim Forest
- *Kersti and Saint Nicholas* – Hilda van Stockum
- *Mary, the Mother of Jesus* – Tomie dePaola
- *Our Lady of Guadalupe* – Tomie dePaola
- *Mary, Mother of Jesus* – Alison Wisenfeld and Mary Joslin
- *Brigid's Cloak* – Bryce Milligan
- *Lucia Saint of Light* – Katherine Bolger Hyde
- *24 Christmas Stories to Welcome Jesus*
- *The Donkey's Dream* – Barbara Helen Berger
- *The Night of Las Posadas* – Tomie dePaola
- *The First Christmas* (pop-up book) – Tomie dePaola
- *The Legend of the Poinsettia* – Tomie dePaola
- *The Friendly Beasts* - Tomie dePaola
- *St. Francis and the Nativity* – Myrna Strasser
- *The Story of Christmas* – George Brundage
- *The Christmas Miracle of Jonathan Toomey* – Susan Wojciechowski
- *The Cobweb Curtain* – Jenny Koralek
- *The Nativity* – Ruth Sanderson

Books for Adults

- *Reflections during Advent* – Dorothy Day
- *Jesus of Nazareth: The Infancy Narratives* – Pope Benedict XVI
- *Advent and Christmas Wisdom from Pope John Paul II* – Complied by John V. Kruse
- *Advent Meditations with Fulton J. Sheen*
- *In Conversation with God – Vol. 1 – Advent and Christmas*
- *The Everlasting Man* – G.K. Chesterton
- *On the Incarnation* – St. Athanasius
- *Sermons for Christmas and Epiphany* – St. Augustine
- *Waiting for Christ* – John Henry Newman
- *Come, Lord Jesus – Meditations on the Art of Waiting* – Mother Mary Frances, P.C.C.
- *Redemptoris Mater* – Encyclical by John Paul II
- *The Blessings of Christmas* – Cardinal Joseph Ratzinger
- *The Catholic All Year Compendium – Liturgical Living for Real Life* – Kendra Tierney

Index of Recipes

(by alphabetical order)

Arroz Dulce 39
Barm Brack 83
Bishopwyn 19
Blanc Mange 65
Brioche 36
Cassata 38
Children's Punch 70
Christmas Lady Cookies 41
Christollen 36
Corn Tortillas 24
Cranberry Muffins 39
Eggnog 41
Initial Cookies 70
Leissi Katter (St. Lucy's Cats) 28
Melachrino 37
Plum Pudding 7
Potica 42
Rum Sauce 8
Sopapillas 25
Speculaas Cookies 19
St. John's Wine 64
St. Nicholas' Purse Cookies 20
Twelfth Night Cake 75

Index of Recipes
(by feast)

Advent
Plum Pudding 7
Rum Sauce 8

St. Nicholas
Bishopwyn 19
Speculaas 19
St. Nicholas' Purse Cookies 20

Our Lady of Guadalupe
Corn Tortillas 24
Sopapillas 25

St. Lucy
Leissi Katter (St. Lucy's Cats) 28

Christmas
Brioche 36
Christollen 36
Melachrino 37
Cassata 38
Arroz Dulce 39
Cranberry Muffins 39
Christmas Lady Cookies 41
Eggnog 41
Potica 42

St. John
St. John's Wine 64

Holy Innocents
Blanc Mange 65

Solemnity of Mary
Children's Punch 70

Initial Cookies 70

Epiphany
Twelfth Night Cake 75

St. Brigid
Barm Brack 83

Index of Songs

(by alphabetical order)

Alma Redeptoris Mater 11
Angels from the Realms of Glory 77
As With Gladness Men of Old 78
Buenos Días, Paloma Blanca 27
Earth Has Many a Noble City 79
Gabriel's Message 14
Hark! The Herald Angels Sing 58
In Deepest Winter 60
Lo, How a Rose E'er Blooming 59
Lully, Lullay (Coventry Carol) 66
Mañanitas a La Virgen de Guadalupe 26
O Come, All Ye Faithful 56
O Come, O Come Emmanuel 12
O Who Loves Nicholas the Saintly 21
Rorate Caeli 13
Savior of the Nations Come 15
Songs of Thankfulness and Praise 80
The Annunciation 30
The Shepherds 56
The Trip to Bethlehem 31
The Wise Men 81
The Word was Made Flesh 71
Ubi Caritas et Amor 68

Index of Songs
(by feast)

Advent
Alma Redeptoris Mater 11
O Come, O Come Emmanuel 12
Rorate Caeli 13
Gabriel's Message 14
Savior of the Nations Come 15
The Annunciation 30
The Trip to Bethlehem 31

St. Nicholas
O Who Loves Nicholas the Saintly 21

Our Lady of Guadalupe
Mañanitas a La Virgen de Guadalupe 26
Buenos Días, Paloma Blanca 27

Christmas
The Shepherds 56
O Come, All Ye Faithful 56
Hark! The Herald Angels Sing 58
Lo, How a Rose E'er Blooming 59
In Deepest Winter 60
Lully, Lullay (Coventry Carol) 66
Ubi Caritas et Amor 68
The Word was Made Flesh 71

Epiphany
Angels from the Realms of Glory 77
As With Gladness Men of Old 78
Earth Has Many a Noble City 79
Songs of Thankfulness and Praise 80
The Wise Men 81

www.ingramcontent.com/pod-product-compliance
Lightning Source LLC
Chambersburg PA
CBHW031159160426
43193CB00008B/436